The Witness of Religion
in an Age of Fear

The Witness of Religion in an Age of Fear

Michael Kinnamon

WESTMINSTER
JOHN KNOX PRESS
LOUISVILLE · KENTUCKY

First edition
Published by Westminster John Knox Press
Louisville, Kentucky

17 18 19 20 21 22 23 24 25 26—10 9 8 7 6 5 4 3 2 1

Book design by Sharon Adams
Cover design by Barbara LeVan Fisher, www.levanfisherstudio.com

Library of Congress Cataloging-in-Publication Data

Names: Kinnamon, Michael, author.
Title: The witness of religion in an age of fear / Michael Kinnamon.
Description: Louisville, KY : Westminster John Knox Press, 2017. | Includes bibliographical references.
Identifiers: LCCN 2016041532 (print) | LCCN 2016042364 (ebook) | ISBN 9780664262020 (pbk. : alk. paper) | ISBN 9781611648027 (ebk.)
Subjects: LCSH: Fear--Religious aspects. | Fear--United States.
Classification: LCC BL65.F4 K56 2017 (print) | LCC BL65.F4 (ebook) | DDC 201/.615246--dc23
LC record available at https://lccn.loc.gov/2016041532

Most Westminster John Knox Press books are available at special quantity discounts when purchased in bulk by corporations, organizations, and special-interest groups. For more information, please e-mail SpecialSales@wjkbooks.com.

"The enemy is fear. We think it is hate; but it is fear."

Mahatma Gandhi

"Do not be afraid. We live in a time when this biblical refrain cannot be repeated too often. . . . Among all the things the church has to say to the world today, this may be the most important."

Scott Bader-Saye

Contents

Preface

In this book, I am making a case that I hope will move all of us to action. Contemporary American society is saturated with fear, fear that is often out of proportion to the actual threats we face. Such excessive fearfulness leads to attacks on the wrong targets and to the misdirecting of finite public resources. It turns suspicion into a virtue, thus making it harder to interact constructively with others.

What I am arguing is that the major world religions all warn about the dangers of excessive fear. Religions as different as Islam and Buddhism, Christianity and Sikhism, Judaism and Hinduism teach ways of overcoming fear, or at least of putting it in proper perspective. This means that people of faith have an important word to say to a fearful culture. And it is my fervent hope that we who are people of faith will increasingly make this witness together.

This book is not intended as a study of comparative religion—although I have tried to make my descriptions of the various traditions, while necessarily brief, as accurate and sympathetic as possible. Nor is this intended as a sociological analysis of contemporary America—although I hope readers will recognize a significant trait of this society in my depiction of it. Rather, this is a call, issued by a professing Christian, to interfaith engagement in the United States. The prevalence of fear is a hazard to our public health about which people of religious faith need to speak out.

I have written this book, for better or worse, during a US presidential campaign marked by a great deal of fear-tinged rhetoric and public anger toward those who are "other"—often an expression of deep-rooted fear. Given the ideological passions of this historical moment, I have little doubt that this book will be read by some as politically partisan, especially since one presidential candidate in particular painted a fearful picture of the contemporary world.

So it needs to be said as clearly as possible: Fear-mongering is by no means limited to one political party, and neither major US party has a monopoly on how to reduce public anxiety. My intent is not to disparage political parties but to rouse religious communities. We need to relearn our teachings about fear and to make these teachings known, alongside neighbors who adhere to other faiths. That itself would be a counterwitness to persons and parties in this country who are apprehensive about welcoming those who are different.

I want to thank all those persons in Missouri, Oklahoma, Washington, and California who heard my presentations of research on this topic. Your questions and comments were an important part of the writing process. My special thanks go to Imam Sayed Moustafa al-Qazwini, Imam Taha Hassane, Thanissaro Bhikkhu, Rabbi Steve Gutow, and Dr. David Scott for contributing to my knowledge of religious traditions other than my own. Of course, any deficiencies in my description of these religions are entirely my own.

This book is dedicated to my granddaughter, Amala, whose name means "pure" in Sanskrit and "hope" in Arabic. May her name increasingly describe the world in which she grows and blossoms.

Introduction

Fear as Blessing and Threat

In March of 2011, the House Homeland Security
Committee, chaired by Rep. Peter King of New York,
launched the first of its hearings into the "extent of
radicalization in the American Muslim community and that community's response." In the weeks preceding the hearings, Rep.
King had repeatedly declared that "85 percent of the mosques
in this country are controlled by Islamic fundamentalists"—
"radicals" who constitute "an enemy living amongst us"—and
that US Muslims have not done nearly enough to help law
enforcement officials identify and stop potential terrorists.[1]

Such claims had already been refuted by, among others,
FBI director Robert Mueller, who in 2008 told the House
Judiciary Committee that "99.9 percent of American Muslims
. . . are every bit as patriotic as anybody else in this room, and
that many of our cases are the result of cooperation from the
Muslim community in the United States."[2] This last point was
corroborated by a Duke University study that concluded that
"the largest single source of initial information" in helping prevent terrorist attacks was members of the Muslim community.[3]
Reporters have determined that Rep. King's assertions were

1

based on an unsubstantiated comment made by one person at a State Department forum in 1999.

I was in the room in the Cannon House Office Building for the opening of these hearings, and, as general secretary of the National Council of Churches, was one of several religious leaders to speak at a subsequent press conference. Together we deplored the focus on a single religious community. After all, as one colleague pointed out, the deadliest act of terrorism on American soil prior to 9/11 (if you don't count the decimation of Native Americans, the enslavement of Africans, and the murderous actions of such groups as the KKK) was the bombing in Oklahoma City perpetrated by a European American who was raised Roman Catholic. Together we protested that representatives of the country's most prominent Muslim organizations were not invited to testify at the hearing.

What struck me most forcefully, however, was that leaders from a wide range of religions—Jews, Muslims, Sikhs, Unitarians, Christians—all noted how fear was driving this process. Domestic terrorism is a real threat, I said at the press conference, but when fear dominates our public decision making, it leads us to focus on easy, surrogate targets rather than on real, complex problems. (This is, unfortunately, true of other nations as well. In Switzerland, for example, a needed debate on immigration and national character got sidetracked by legislation banning the building of minarets.[4]) Furthermore, I argued, these fear-driven congressional hearings stoke unwarranted suspicion in the American public ("If Congress is investigating, there must be good reason"), which, in turn, increases the level of anxiety among US Muslims. My colleagues and I agreed that such excessive, cumulative fearfulness is dangerous, not only to the Islamic community, but to America as a whole. And it is contrary to the core teachings of our religions.

A Complex Topic

Fear has a legitimate, even vital, role to play in human society. Indeed, without this elemental alarm system, our ancestors would not have survived, and we would not be warned of potential dangers or sufficiently motivated to address them. Fear can move us to marshal our resources in the face of crisis; and there *are* real crises, genuine threats, in this obviously troubled world. As I write this, there are certainly good reasons why religious minorities in Iraq and Syria or school children in northern Nigeria or residents of low-lying Pacific islands would be afraid. A basic premise of this book, however, is that fear, when it becomes excessive or misdirected, is itself dangerous. It can lead us to misperceive the world around us and can undermine our willingness to interact constructively with others. In the words of President Obama, "Fear can lead us to lash out against those who are different, or lead us to try to get some sinister 'other' under control. Alternatively, fear can lead us to succumb to despair or paralysis or cynicism. Fear can feed our more selfish impulses, and erode the bonds of community. . . . [I]t can be contagious, spreading through societies, and through nations. And if we let it consume us, the consequences of that fear can be worse than any outward threat."[5]

Martin Luther King Jr., a man who lived with daily threat, said it memorably: "Normal fear protects us; abnormal fear paralyzes us. Normal fear motivates us to improve our individual and collective welfare; abnormal fear constantly poisons and distorts our inner lives."[6] I saw clearly at the congressional hearing how fear has the potential to turn people against their neighbors, corroding the trust and interdependence on which society depends. There are times of crisis when fear can unite a community; but history teaches that more often it divides.

Having said this, I want to underscore that fear is a complex topic. Part of that complexity is on full display in the highly acclaimed book by Ta-Nehisi Coates, *Between the World and Me*. Growing up in Baltimore, writes Coates,

> the only people I knew were black, and all of them were powerfully, adamantly, dangerously afraid. . . . To be black in the Baltimore of my youth was to be naked before the elements of the world, before all the guns, fists, knives, crack, rape,

and disease. The nakedness was not an error, nor pathology.
The nakedness is the correct and intended result of policy,
the predictable upshot of people forced for centuries to live
under fear. The law did not protect us.[7]

Often this fear is transmuted into rage—"violence rose from
the fear like smoke from a fire"[8]—which compounds the threat
to others in the black community. According to a report from
the Bureau of Justice Statistics, between 1976 and 2005, the
homicide rate was 4.8 per 100,000 for white Americans, but a
stomach-turning 36.9 for blacks![9] In some neighborhoods in
this nation, fear is endemic, part of a cycle that has its roots in
a history of systemic oppression.

As a white Christian man born in the United States who
is not poor, I have not faced a daily fear of gang violence or
deportation. I have not known the fear that comes from the
danger of sexual assault. I have not seen my religion treated as
a public threat. I have not felt the gnawing insecurity of having to decide between spending money for food or medical
insurance. So it is not for me, or others like me, to dismiss as
illegitimate or destructive these fears that many Americans live
with every day. What I do want to suggest, however, is that
oppressive, discriminatory actions are themselves often born of
fear—as we have seen, for example, in the killings of unarmed
black men by fearful white police. Even worse, fear is a tool
regularly used by those with power to keep others down. "[T]o
be forced to live in fear," says Coates, "[is] a great injustice."[10]
In this book, I want to call our attention to the fear that causes
others to be afraid.

This book does not break new ground in identifying fear as
a dominant theme in the public life of contemporary America.
Several scholars have written persuasively about "the culture of
fear" in this country, and I will draw extensively on their work,
especially in chapter 1. Some of these scholars contend that
the United States is more fearful in this era than in many previous ones; others maintain that what we are witnessing today is

simply the continuation of entrenched cultural patterns. I will leave that for them to debate. My concern is to emphasize that fear, here and now, is often misdirected (as in the congressional hearing) and that, in the nation as a whole, the level of fear is out of sync with our actual situation. For example, surveys taken over the past two decades consistently show that, while crime rates are falling dramatically, the fear of crime is high and generally rising. It is an indication, as many have noted, that the country is in the grip of a collective apprehension that can distort public priorities and decision making, to the great detriment of many of its citizens.

What may be new is my contention that religions, at their best, have not only a word of comfort for those who are afraid, but also a word of challenge for those who manipulate fear to their own advantage or who succumb to such manipulation. People of faith are by no means the only ones who know that fear can be hazardous to social well-being, but they (we) do have, I believe, a vital role to play in naming and responding to the problem.

This argument may seem counterintuitive to some, since religion and fear often seem to go hand in hand. Bertrand Russell, in his famous critique of religion, makes two points that are difficult to refute: (1) Religious belief, for many people, is motivated by a fear of forces beyond their control, including illness and death. "It is partly," writes Russell, "the terror of the unknown and partly . . . the wish to feel that you have a kind of elder brother who will stand by you in all your troubles and disputes."[11] (2) Religion also engenders fear when it teaches divine punishment for sinful behavior, both in this life and the next. The language of Jonathan Edwards's famous sermon "Sinners in the Hands of an Angry God" ("You hang by a slender thread, with the flames of divine wrath flashing about it") may no longer be in fashion, but the underlying theology still has a hold on many believers and continues to be used as a motivation for religious conversion. Christianity, in particular, also has an apocalyptic strand that forecasts a terrifying end to the world itself—a belief that proved astonishingly popular in the last decades of the twentieth century.

The connection between religion and fear seems particularly apparent in an era when fundamentalist religion captures the headlines. Nearly all of the major world religions have their fundamentalist wings; and fundamentalism, whatever its veneer, is the religious form of the world's anxiety. It draws lines, to keep its identity secure by keeping others out. It responds to anxiety by demanding certainty, which leaves no room to consider views at variance with its own. It adopts a mindset of scarcity (if you win, I lose) and thus assumes that the goal is to defeat or convert those who are "other." There is no doubt that many fearful things have been done, and are being done today, in the name of religion seen through such a lens.[12]

I don't mean to suggest, however, that fear of others is associated only with fundamentalism. Polls in the United States show that churchgoers in general are more likely than the public as a whole to favor restrictions on civil liberties and immigration and to countenance the use of torture in the name of promoting security.[13] My argument, therefore, is more prescriptive than descriptive. I am convinced that the major world religions can be—and should be—a bulwark against obsessive, excessive fear. I have no desire to harmonize religious teachings; differences are often as interesting and important as similarities. But I hope to demonstrate in chapters 2 and 3 that people of faith—including Christians, Jews, Muslims, Buddhists, Hindus, Bahá'ís, and Sikhs—when true to their central traditions, all affirm Gandhi's insight that "the enemy is fear. We think it is hate; but it is fear"—because fear is so often the root of hatred.

The responses to fear in these various religions, while by no means identical, all seek to put fear in proper perspective, even to overcome it, by seeking security only in God or in freedom from worldly attachments. In chapter 5, I will make the case that people of faith, for all of their differences, should together challenge the assumptions of a fearful culture.

In short, this book is a call to religious renewal—trust in the Holy One, in Ultimate Reality, should be an antidote to fear in human society, not a cause of it—and a call to interfaith collaboration. Together we have a word for a time such as this!

Fear and Anxiety

Throughout this book, "fear" and "anxiety" will at times be used interchangeably. There is, however, an important distinction between them: "fear" is generally used in connection with a specific, immediate, objective threat, while "anxiety" is used when the threat is more anticipated than immediate, more generalized than specific, more subjective (an inner state) than objective and external. Anxiety received increased attention in the first half of the twentieth century because of its use in the vocabulary of the psychological sciences. The term became nearly ubiquitous with the publication of W. H. Auden's famous poem "The Age of Anxiety" in 1947, followed by Leonard Bernstein's symphony of the same name (1949) and Rollo May's best-selling book *The Meaning of Anxiety* in 1950.

This distinction between anxiety and fear is not always easy to maintain. Terrorism, for example, may be an imminent fear in one place or time, but a generalized, nonspecific anxiety at another. The distinction becomes useful, however, when we realize, in the words of theologian Paul Tillich, that "[a]nxiety strives to become fear, because fear can be met by courage."[14] To say it another way, people have difficulty living with unspecified anxiety; and so they look for a definite object of their fear—a group, a person, a movement—that can be analyzed, attacked, or avoided. As the congressional hearings indicate, a somewhat amorphous anxiety regarding terrorism can become focused in the fear of Muslims. A free-floating anxiety over the changing demographics of US society finds outlet in a fear of immigrants and refugees—Mexicans and Central Americans at one moment, Middle Easterners at another. This, some argue, helps explain the current prevalence of fear language. Others contend that the real source of the present culture of fear is those groups in American society—the media, politicians, corporations—that profit from it. We will make further mention of such theories in the next chapter.

I will end this introduction by returning to a paradox hinted at above: fearful people make others afraid! The French scholar Dominique Moïsi, in his insightful look at this country, suggests that "there is one America united by fear and another united by the fear of fear."[15] Surveys indicate, for example, that roughly 40 percent of Americans report having a gun in their home, usually for reasons of personal security, while equal numbers find that statistic downright scary. Similarly, a nation that fearfully prizes military security above other priorities, including civil rights, makes me and many others afraid for its future.

The greatest paradox, however, would be if the effect of this book were to add fear to the list of things to be afraid of! My purpose is not to make readers afraid of fear. It is, rather, a call to action, especially for people of religious faith. We have resources in our sacred traditions that can counter the fear that is so rampant in contemporary America—if only we will identify and use them.

1

The Culture of Fear in Contemporary America

As I prepared to write this chapter, news broke of terrorist attacks in Paris: at least 129 persons murdered by ISIS-inspired extremists in six locations around a city that is a symbol of Western culture. It was an awful, frightening event that created understandable anxiety across France and other European nations.

The response in this country, however, was more troubling—an example of what several commentators called "the politics of fear." In direct reaction to the Paris attacks, the House of Representatives, with bipartisan support, voted to tighten already-stringent screening requirements for Syrian refugees, while a majority of governors announced their opposition to receiving Syrian refugees in their states. "Texas," said Gov. Greg Abbott, "will not accept any Syrian refugees, and I demand the United States act similarly. Security comes first."[1] This despite the fact that all of the Paris assailants were citizens of European Union countries and that, of the nearly 785,000 refugees admitted through the US Refugee Admissions Program since 9/11, "only about a dozen," in the words of a State Department spokesperson, "have been arrested or removed from the United States due to terrorism concerns that existed prior to their resettlement in the U.S. None of them were Syrian."[2] Seth Jones, director of the International Security and Defense Policy Center at the RAND Corporation, put it this way in his testimony to Congress in June 2015: "The threat to the U.S. homeland from refugees [in general] has been relatively low. Almost none of the major terrorist plots since 9/11 have involved refugees. Even in those cases where refugees were arrested on terrorism-related charges, years and even decades often transpired between their entry into the United States and their involvement in terrorism. In most instances, a would-be terrorist's refugee status had little or nothing to do with their radicalization and shift to terrorism."[3]

In the aftermath of the Paris killings, the *New York Times* editorial board warned of "the danger of self-inflicted injury" when our nation reacts out of fear. It is hard not to agree with their conclusion: "In our time, disastrous things have been done in the name of safety."[4]

I do not mean to impugn the motives of those who claim to speak and act out of a desire to protect Americans. Terrorism is a real threat to be taken seriously; sincere, informed people can disagree on the appropriate response to it. But, as many have pointed out, a misdirected, fear-driven response can itself be a threat to national security. "They [ISIS] can't beat us on the battlefield," said President Obama, "so they try to terrorize us into being afraid, into changing our patterns of behavior, into abandoning our allies and partners, into retreating from the world."[5] The Islamic State knows it cannot topple the French or American government with terrorist assaults, said French philosopher and psychoanalyst Hélène L'Heuillet, in an interview following the events in Paris. For them, "it is not important to win. It is important to scare."[6] In this regard, the Paris attacks, like the attacks of 9/11, have succeeded, perhaps beyond what even the terrorists would have imagined.

The horrific tragedy of September 11, 2001, did not create our national anxiety. Scholars, as we shall see, were already speaking of our "culture of fear" prior to 9/11. But this event, as well as the response to it, surely exacerbated public fearfulness.[7] Rather than target those who planned and executed the attacks, the US government universalized the response into a war against terror (complete with color-coded terror alerts) that reflects a high level of anxiety and is guaranteed to keep people afraid.

David Rothkopf, editor of the journal *Foreign Policy*, argues that "the country has crossed the fine line that separates national security from national *in*security. Fear now seems to drive more of the country's policies than the vision, self-awareness, and courage that used to be the recipe for protecting and advancing U.S. interests internationally."[8] Rothkopf acknowledges that there are real threats in this world, but in our anxiety, he writes, we have "redefined disproportionate," in the name of security enacting policies that have massively expanded domestic surveillance, undercut fundamental civil liberties, authorized (for several years) the use of torture, alienated vital allies, and spent trillions of dollars that might have gone for other pressing priorities.[9]

Peter Stearns, a professor of history at George Mason University, supports the idea that America is suffering "the social equivalent of a panic attack" by comparing the US response to 9/11 to major terrorist incidents in Spain and Britain, where the public mood, by most accounts, was not so much fearful as defiant. "The only organized effort to stay out of public places after the London attack," he notes, "came from American military bases, where personnel were confined to quarters until British annoyance prompted a reversal of policy."[10] Stearns admits that the comparison is imprecise, since the devastation and loss of life were considerably less than in the United States in 2001; but the difference in public attitude is still revealing.

Another comparison Stearns offers is historical. In the weeks following the attack on Pearl Harbor, more than two hundred Americans from across the nation were interviewed regarding their response to that event. Even though there was a specific question concerning fear, the responses showed virtually no expression of the emotion. Rather, the persons interviewed "expressed great confidence that, despite the lack of preparedness, their government would be able to handle the problem."[11] Stearns contrasts this with stories submitted to a 9/11 website where fear reactions predominated. Again, there are important caveats. Hawaii, far away from most Americans, in 1941 was not yet a state, and most of the deaths were military. I suspect, however, that the comparison will ring true for many readers.

I certainly do not want to minimize the pain and loss stemming from any death at the hands of terrorists. ISIS can be particularly frightening, because its brutal violence is indiscriminate. It is important, however, to put the threat of terrorism in some perspective. From 9/11 through the end of 2015, forty-five persons were killed in the United States as a result of jihadist violence, most of them in the attacks at Fort Hood and San Bernardino.[12] More have died at the hands of white supremacists, antigovernment fanatics, or other non-Muslim extremists—which is why a survey of police and sheriff's departments nationwide found that 74 percent of them listed antigovernment, not jihadist, violence as the greatest threat to public safety.[13] A 2013 report by the National Consortium for the Study of Terrorism and Responses to Terrorism points out that terrorist attacks, attempted and successful, have become *less* frequent in the United States since the 1970s (with the huge exception of 9/11) and that the odds of an American being killed in such an attack, either in this country or overseas, are minuscule: roughly 1 in 20 million. The odds of drowning in a bathtub: 1 in 800,000. Dying in a car crash: 1 in 19,000. A person is nearly four times as likely to die by being hit by lightning.[14]

There is a sense, of course, in which such statistics are misleading. Terrorism is an act of deliberate malice and carries with it the risk of another 9/11-sized massacre. It is appropriate to be prudent, even when the risk is low. Still, when 49 percent of Americans in a 2015 Gallup survey[15] reported being very or somewhat fearful that they or a member of their family will become a victim of terrorism, it would seem that the level of national anxiety is greatly out of sync with the actual danger. The country, as Rothkopf suggests, is in a difficult cycle: "disproportionate" government policies and rhetoric feed the public's fearfulness, even as our fearfulness encourages the expansion of these policies. Being afraid, the nation has set up an incredibly elaborate security apparatus that now has a stake in keeping the public perpetually afraid.

The financial cost of this longing for security is astonishing. In the decade after 9/11, the United States spent nearly $8 trillion on the Pentagon's base budget, the cost of war, and the apparatus of homeland security—far more than that spent by all the rest of the world.[16] Our defense budget alone, even with recent reductions, remains larger than the next eight highest-spending countries combined.[17] What Timothy Egan calls the "fear-industrial complex" so dominates national priorities that, by one estimate, the United States spends $500 million per victim of terrorism but only $10,000 per cancer death. Egan notes that Alzheimer's kills more than eighty thousand Americans a year, but the total 2014 federal research budget for Alzheimer's through the National Institutes of Health was a mere $562 million.[18] It is, of course, impossible to know how many lives might have been lost to terrorism without the massive expenditure on security. But given the relative prevalence of other risks, it seems clear that fear of terrorism has distorted political decision making, to the detriment of the country as a whole.

However, as great as the financial cost may be, the cost to America's reputation as a place of welcome and opportunity, and as a model of democratic tolerance, is even greater. "America," writes the insightful analyst Fareed Zakaria, "has become a nation consumed by anxiety, worried about terrorists and rogue nations, Muslims and Mexicans, foreign companies and free trade, immigrants and international organizations. The strongest nation in the history of the world now sees itself as besieged by forces beyond its control."[19] With regard to the reception of immigrants and refugees, an area in which the United States has been a model for others, "the country has regressed toward an angry, defensive crouch"[20]—an observation written before the temperature of our fear reached its current level.

Once again, other countries provide a telling contrast. Sweden, for example, agreed to take nearly two hundred thousand refugees in 2015, many of them from war zones in the Middle East. "Plenty of Swedes told me," says James Traub, a fellow at the Center for International Cooperation, "that they didn't believe their country could integrate all those newcomers, but scarcely anyone mentioned the alleged terrorist threat from refugees. They were worried, but they were not frightened."[21]

And then there is Canada—a nation that too has suffered from a terrorist attack in its capital—which pledged to receive twenty-five thousand Syrian refugees within three months, with its prime minister telling the first planeload to arrive, "You're safe at home now." It is a far cry from the howls of fear-tinged protest that greeted President Obama's plan to resettle ten thousand, after strenuous vetting, over the course of a year. Writes Traub: "The towers fell more than fourteen years ago; the statute of limitations on post-9/11 panic has expired. Yet Americans have never been more fearful."[22] The mood most characteristic of this nation has historically been a self-confidence bordering on arrogance. Now it is fear.

A Culture of Fear

The extraordinary level of often-misdirected anxiety surrounding national security and immigration is part of a larger cultural pattern pointed to by sociologists. One of the first to sound the alarm about the nation's state of alarm was Barry Glassner in his book of 1999 (updated a decade later), *The Culture of Fear: Why Americans Are Afraid of the Wrong Things*. Glassner details a series of overblown—in some cases, completely unwarranted—fears that have grabbed public attention, many of them having to do with crime—including workplace assaults, poisoned Halloween candy, cyberpredators, and abductions of children by strangers.[23]

Glassner is certainly not the only one to note that American's fear of crime is incredibly out of sync with reality. The rate of crime in general, and violent crime in particular, has come down significantly since the early 1990s. According to the FBI's 2014 crime report, violent crime was down 16.2 percent from a decade earlier. Rape was down 10.9 percent over than same period, robbery down 22 percent, aggravated assault down 14 percent, and murder down 20.8 percent. In 2014, there were 14,249 murders in the United States, obviously still too high but the lowest number since 1968, when the country had nearly 120 million fewer residents.[24] The overall crime rate in 2015 is half of what it was in 1990.[25] Since crimes are disproportionately concentrated in certain parts of the population, most Americans are far safer now than at any other time in the history of this nation.

At the same time, however, Gallup surveys consistently show that more than half of the persons polled say that the nation's crime problem is extremely or very serious, and two-thirds think it is getting worse. Almost four in ten say they would not feel safe walking alone at night near where they live.[26]

Of course, statistics are no consolation for a victim who suffers the pain and loss and residual fear associated with violent crime. Still, it needs to be stressed that the anxious misperception of the prevalence of crime has negative consequences for the society as a whole. One of these is the astonishingly high level of incarceration. In 2014, the United States had 743 prisoners for every 100,000 citizens, while the average worldwide was 148.[27] Nearly a quarter of all prisoners across the globe are behind bars in this country (which has 4.4 percent of the world's population). Eighteen states now spend more on jails and prisons than on colleges and universities, a striking indication that fear has triumphed over hope in political decision making.[28]

Another remarkable dimension of contemporary American society tied to the misplaced fear of crime is gun ownership. The United States has *by far* the highest number of privately owned firearms, and the highest rate of private gun ownership, of any nation. Americans have nearly 50 percent more guns per capita than the next most heavily armed country, Yemen.[29] When asked why they own a gun, 60 percent of Americans say it is for personal safety and protection—despite the fact that "violent victimization by strangers," the sort of crime people arm themselves against, has fallen 77 percent in the past quarter century.[30] I agree with philosophy professor Firmin DeBrabander when he writes, "Guns do not liberate us from fear. They are a symptom of fear's domination over society. The gun-rights movement capitalizes on fear wherever it resides in our culture, and drums it up to amazing heights"[31]—a point we will return to shortly.

This discussion of crime takes us again to the topic of race, since, in the minds of many whites, "black" is associated with criminality. The Roman Catholic priest Bryan Massingale, who is African American, has written of his despondency, laced with anger, at the "not guilty" verdict in the death of Trayvon Martin: "Because too often I also have been saddled with the responsibility for managing white people's fear and anxiety, charged with going the extra mile to assure them that I am not a threat. . . . For them, it is a self-evident fact that the vast majority of crimes are committed by black males—despite the empirical evidence to the contrary."[32]

The columnist Alexandra Petri makes the connection with the theme of this book even more explicitly:

> You could smell fear all over the story of Trayvon Martin. . . . Fear of the nameless, faceless menace of You Shouldn't Be Here. It's the fear that makes someone appoint himself neighborhood watchman in the first place, to make sure nothing Out of Place shows up. . . . Fortunately for the fearful, Florida's "Stand Your Ground" law has their interests at

heart. To kill someone, you need not prove that he or she intended you harm. All you need prove is a real and reasonable fear that your life is in danger.[33]

Petri concludes, "We live in a terrified age." Her judgment is reinforced by the now-familiar story from Ferguson, Missouri, with its images of police decked out as if for military invasion, and by the tension, driven by fear on both sides, between police and African Americans across the country. The matter was poignantly expressed by Kellon Nixon, who, with his young son, took part in the Dallas protest march in July 2016 against the police shooting of black men in Baton Rouge and Minneapolis. That protest was tragically disrupted when a sniper killed five policemen who were protecting the protesters. In response to a reporter's question, Nixon insisted that he was not afraid: "Being afraid only causes a person to act irrationally. And I think this is one of the biggest problems between African Americans and the police, that we are both afraid of one another, and so we act irrationally."[34]

Fear is not, of course, a new theme in American history. There have been periods of excessive, misdirected anxiety, from the Salem witch trials to popular images of "savages" on the frontier, from the antiforeigner hysteria—the so-called "Red Scare"—of the early 1920s to the McCarthyism and bomb shelters of the 1950s. Many readers will know the language of President Franklin Roosevelt: "[T]he only thing we have to fear is fear itself—nameless, unreasoning, unjustified terror which paralyzes needed efforts to convert retreat into advance." It is a reminder of how fear had gripped the country as a result of the Great Depression.

What I am suggesting is that we are today in the midst of another period in which fear dominates our national psyche—a claim that, as we have seen, is supported by the work of numerous scholars. The British sociologist Frank Furedi, author of *The Politics of Fear*, goes so far as to argue that a "narrative of fear" has become the framework through which

Western societies interpret public experiences, leading to nations marked increasingly by security systems, gated communities, public surveillance, and a steady diet of media stories about dangers immediate or potential.

This narrative of fear has become so internalized, contends Furedi, that being frightened is no longer necessarily linked to a specific threat. Vulnerability has now become an identity, an inherent condition of an individual or group, "a culturally sanctioned affectation that pervades all aspects of life."[35] The problem, to put it another way, is not that we have fears (some of which may well be warranted), but that we live in a *state* of fear that affects the way we see the world, creating anxiety that is not in proportion to actual danger. Do vaccinations cause autism? Will this season's flu become a pandemic? Will this food make me sick? Will this toy hurt my child? Could that homemade clock really be a bomb?

The Ebola crisis of 2014 is a case in point. A survey taken in the fall of that year found that 43 percent of Americans were afraid they or a member of their immediate family would contract Ebola, at a time when there were *four* laboratory-confirmed cases of the disease in all of the United States.[36] Politicians immediately used this to push other fear buttons. One senator suggested that the Islamic State may use Ebola as a biological weapon, and several congresspersons demanded that the border with Mexico be closed to keep Ebola out—despite the fact that Ebola did not exist in Central or Latin America. As one scholar observes, President Roosevelt's effort to name and subvert the fear of his era "forms an intriguing contrast to more recent American formulations, in which leaders have attempted to encourage and manipulate fears and have systematically avoided opportunities to urge Americans not to be needlessly afraid."[37] We will return to this point more than once.

Why So Much Fear?

What I have presented thus far is by no means an exhaustive treatment of fear in contemporary American culture; but

I trust the basic point is clear. The widely respected novelist Marilynne Robinson puts it succinctly: "Fear has, in this moment, a respectability I've never seen in my life."[38]

Why is this so? I asked this of South African friends after they had spoken of their shock upon moving to the United States and discovering the prevalence of social anxiety. South Africans have more reasons to be afraid, they told a group of us, but Americans seem far more driven by fear. "Perhaps," they suggested, "this is because you haven't had a Nelson Mandela."

There is surely much wisdom in this statement. Leadership can make a significant difference in the public's perception of events—especially the leadership of a person like Mandela, who declared, "The brave man is not he who does not feel afraid, but he who conquers that fear."[39] Our political leaders, it can be argued, have failed to provide inspiring alternatives and to call us to our better nature. This has led to a loss of confidence in the ability of public institutions to respond effectively to crises. I doubt, however, that this is a sufficient explanation, since few countries have leaders like Mandela. Three other theories help me make sense of the current climate of anxiety.

One explanation, especially championed by Peter Stearns, has to do with a change in the socialization process by which children in the United States learn to be adults. Stearns argues that, until the early twentieth century, children, especially boys, were urged not to avoid fear but to overcome it with courage. The development of courage, through at least limited exposure to risk, was regarded as an indispensable part of a person's education, a trait that would enable one to deal constructively with life's inevitable trials. Roosevelt's famous appeal to stand firm in the face of fear was based on this older assumption.

Beginning in the 1920s, however, "experts increasingly recommended that fear as an overpowering emotion . . . must be sidestepped wherever possible, rather than confronted."[40] New research into childrearing suggested that children are emotionally fragile, harboring irrational fears that ought to be addressed through regular reassurance and protection. Stearns is a careful scholar who recognizes the impact of other factors on our "culture of fear"; but he believes that a study of American history confirms his thesis, that we have a surfeit of fear in our society "because of nearly a century of well-intentioned but misguided attempts to sanitize an unavoidable emotion."[41] Having developed unrealistic hopes for risk-free existence, the public overreacts when these are unfulfilled.

A second theory, more widely held, is that, for the first time in two centuries, people in Europe and North America feel that events are out of "our" control. Dominique Moïsi, a founder of the French Institute for International Affairs, summarizes the perceived threat this way: "Asia is about to overtake us economically. Fundamentalists in the Islamic world are intent on destroying us. Immigrants from the southern nations are about to overwhelm us."[42] Each of us, individually, may not have had power, but our nation, our Western civilization, certainly did, and now that sense of secure superiority is eroding. Fear, writes Moïsi, has become "the dominant emotion in the West" because the very identity of Western society is under attack.[43]

British-born historian Tony Judt argues similarly that "we have entered an age of fear" marked by understandable insecurity in the face of terrorism or economic uncertainty and, "perhaps above all, [by] fear that it is not just *we* who can no longer shape our lives but that those in authority have also lost control to forces beyond their reach."[44] In short, we fear rapid, unmanageable change in a world that looks increasingly rudderless and unfamiliar.

This last point is reinforced by a poll conducted by public opinion researchers Chris Jackson and Cliff Young. More than half of the adults surveyed "don't identify with what America has become," and nearly as many agree with the statement "I feel like a stranger in my own country."[45] The percentages were even higher among respondents who identify themselves as Republicans, which may account for the popularity of presidential candidates whose populism speaks to a deep, emotional sense of economic and cultural displacement. Columnist

Michael Gerson suggests that this poll is evidence of "a protest against rapid and disorienting social change, against an increasingly multicultural country"[46]—and it is often manifest in the language of fear.

As I write this, I recall an image from Murrieta, California, where in the summer of 2014 buses of unaccompanied minors and women with children, all fleeing violence in Central America, were blocked by angry, screaming adults.[47] Reflecting on this incident, Jim Wallis, founder and editor of *Sojourners* magazine, told of a talk he gave on immigration to his son's fifth-grade class in Washington, DC—a class that was racially, ethnically, and religiously diverse. He talked about families separated or deported because they were undocumented, and the students wanted to know: Why doesn't the government fix that? They say they are afraid, Wallis told them. What, the students asked, are they afraid of? "Then it hit me. 'They are afraid of you,' I replied. . . . 'They are afraid you are the future of America. They are afraid their country will someday look like this class—that you represent what our nation is becoming.'"[48] Profound social changes, whether loss of international dominance or loss of demographic familiarity, may well account, at least in part, for the current culture of fear.

The third frequently advanced explanation is more insidious: Americans are excessively fearful because it is in the interests of various groups to make and keep us afraid. Of course, fear is, to some extent, innate; our distant ancestors had an instinct to flee in the face of imminent danger. It seems clear, however, that our experience of fear, in Furedi's words, "is also shaped by a cultural script that instructs people on how to respond to threats to their security."[49] What we fear and to what extent we fear it are largely learned. Various studies confirm that our emotional response is often not proportional to the actual threat, because we are strongly influenced by messages from our social context, which leaves people vulnerable to what Furedi calls "fear entrepreneurs."[50]

Glassner puts it this way: "The short answer to why Americans harbor so many misbegotten fears is that immense power and money await those who tap into our moral insecurities and supply us with symbolic substitutes."[51] In Glassner's view, the primary offenders are the news media. Fear sells; fear increases ratings. Thus the public is fed a steady diet of sensationalized stories that play up the sense of threat. He notes, for example, that during the 1990s, when the murder rate in this country declined by 20 percent, the number of murder stories on network newscasts *increased* by 600 percent—and this does not count stories about O. J. Simpson.[52] More recent studies show, in the words of sociologist Valerie Callanan, that "roughly one-third of all television news is comprised of crime-related content, which is overwhelmingly violent and focused on the most *atypical* crime events."[53] A study by the Annenberg Public Policy Center at the University of Pennsylvania confirms that the more people watch local TV news (let alone the plethora of crime-focused dramas), the greater their fear of crime.[54]

To be fair, Glassner also emphasizes that responsible news sources attempt, at times, to counter the fear-mongering practiced by others—for instance, the National Rifle Association. As I write this book, the NRA has released a new video advertisement in which its executive vice president, Wayne LaPierre, warns that "innocents like us will continue to be slaughtered in concert halls, sports stadiums, restaurants, and airplanes. No amount of bloodshed will ever satisfy the demons among us. . . . [These monsters] will come to where we worship, where we educate, and where we live."[55] This bald attempt to incite fear in order to bolster the NRA's opposition to laws aimed at regulating guns has been strongly criticized by numerous media outlets.

Of course, other parts of the media are not so responsible. Glenn Beck, to take only one example from cable news, has made numerous claims about illegal immigrants that are clearly intended to stoke "fear and loathing" in his audience. The following two are from 2007.[56] "It is time we wake up in this country. We are dealing with an illegal alien crime wave, and drug smuggling is just the beginning." Studies conducted by researchers at Harvard University and the University of Michigan prove, to the contrary, that immigrants, including undocumented ones, are less likely to commit crimes than native-born Americans.[57] "I also know our country is on fire, and the fuel is illegal immigration. . . . They put a strain on our Social Security, our education, our health care, and, yes, national security." The truth is that undocumented immigrants are ineligible for nearly all federal programs, including food stamps, Medicaid, and welfare. And they pay more in payroll taxes, including Social Security, than they will ever consume in public benefits.[58]

Then there are the politicians who exaggerate dangers against which only they can protect us, denounce opponents as being too soft on national security or immigration or crime, and focus on external threats in order to deflect attention from other issues. One would think that leaders in the battle against terrorism would strive to lessen the grip of terror. Instead, fear is often manipulated for political purposes.[59]

There have been so many examples of what David Remnick calls "the politics of perpetual fear"[60] in the 2015–16 presidential campaign that I won't attempt to cite them. It is worth noting, however, that this is not a new characteristic of American politics. The only way to maintain the size of the military, now that World War II has ended, said Senator Arthur Vandenberg in the late 1940s, is "to scare the hell out of the American people."[61] Richard Nixon once famously observed, "People react to fear, not love. They don't teach that in Sunday School, but it's true." Studies conducted during the presidency of George W. Bush established a clear correlation between new terror alerts and the president's approval ratings, and between reminders of 9/11 and support for the president[62]—connections not lost on his advisers. Lest anyone think pandering to fear is limited to one end of the political spectrum, recall a famous ad from Hillary Clinton's 2008 campaign. As a telephone rings in the White House, a voice says, "It's 3:00 a.m. and your children are safe and asleep . . . in a dangerous world. Who do you want answering the phone?"

In 2008, much of the voting public indicated that they supported Barack Obama because they thought he could change the national narrative—from fear to hope. I think it is fair to say, however, that the change he promised—and in some sense embodied—made others even more anxious. By 2016 there was a sense among many of his supporters that in certain respects he too had succumbed to the culture of fear that pervades the Capitol.

Of course, if the media use fear to increase viewers or readers, and politicians employ scare tactics to garner support, it is because we the public respond positively to such tactics. Isn't it up to us, including religious communities, to say, "Enough!"?

Misperceiving the Times

As I end this chapter, I want to be sure my argument is not misunderstood. There *are* real reasons, valid reasons, why people might be anxious: about finding or keeping a job, about health care for ourselves or our loved ones, about safety for our children. There *are* threats to the United States and real reasons for world leaders to be concerned: a deteriorating environment, terrorism and civil conflict, far too many people still living in life-stunting poverty, racism and other forms of violence against minorities. In short, there are understandable reasons why people might be afraid.

What I am suggesting, however, is that fear has become the primary lens through which many Americans see contemporary events. This not only has negative social consequences, as noted in this chapter, but blinds us to the positive things happening around us. Let me put it another way: how we read history is an act of interpretation, and there are certainly other ways to interpret the present moment than through the lens of fear.

For example, more than a billion fewer people live in

conditions of extreme poverty today than in 1990. During that same period, more than two billion gained access to improved drinking water, the percentage of undernourished people in developing countries was cut nearly in half, and there was a remarkable reduction in the proportion of the world's population living in urban slums.[63]

On the global health front, new infections of HIV fell by one-third between 2000 and 2012, mortality rates from malaria decreased by more than 25 percent during the past decade, and the mortality rate for children under five dropped by 41 percent between 1990 and 2011. Educationally, the number of children out of school has declined by almost half since 2000, while the gender gap in primary education has closed in almost every country. *And*, despite the awful, headline-grabbing violence in such places as Syria and Afghanistan, levels of interstate and societal warfare are lower than at any point since the early 1960s.[64]

To put it succinctly, fewer children are starving and dying of disease, and more are in school, than at any time in recorded history.[65] "It is now possible," writes Michael Gerson, "to set goals in a number of areas—malaria elimination, an AIDS-free generation, the end of extreme poverty—and not be dismissed as a crank,"[66] or to read contemporary history through a lens of hope rather than fear without being dismissed as naive or foolish. Yet a 2013 survey of Americans found that 66 percent think the share of the world's population living in absolute poverty has doubled in the past two decades, and another 29 percent think it hasn't changed[67]—pessimistic perceptions that are completely at odds with the facts.

The picture looks the same when we focus on the United States, as Daniel Gardiner documents in his book *The Science of Fear*. In 1900, he points out, nearly 20 percent of all children born in this country died before they were five years old; by the beginning of this century, the percentage was 0.8. Over the past century the portion of the average family's budget going toward food has fallen from 44 percent to around 15 percent.

In Gardiner's words, "We are the healthiest, wealthiest, and longest-lived people in history. And we are increasingly afraid. This is one of the great paradoxes of our time. . . . It seems the less we have to fear, the more we fear."[68] It is not Pollyannaish to give thanks that the mortality rate in the United States for the two leading causes of death—heart disease and cancer— has moved steadily downward over the past twenty-five years. And it is not cantankerous to lament that such developments receive little attention from the major news outlets.

Danny Westneat, a columnist for the *Seattle Times*, makes this argument even more immediate in a column marking the end of 2014.[69] When compared to the previous year, he observes, unemployment was down, the budget deficit was down, oil imports and gas prices were down, the number of medically uninsured was down, violent crime was down, military casualties were down, teen pregnancies were down, the school dropout rate was down, the numbers of divorces and abortions were down—but the number of people saying they were afraid for the future of the country was up 21 percent. It is a striking indication of how fear has shaped the national narrative, further abetted by the near-apocalyptic tone of recent political rhetoric: "Our country is going to hell." America is headed for the "cliff to oblivion." "The patient is the United States of America, and the patient is in critical condition." "Our nation is under siege. What I believe we're facing is the next world war."[70] Politicians seem to be distinguished by what they claim Americans should fear the most.

As we have seen, this narrative of fear can lead us as a nation to misperceive the world around us, to focus our anxiety on false targets, and to deny the interdependence so essential to human community. Perhaps even worse for persons of faith, it can cause us to miss the astonishing, hopeful things God may be doing right now to promote fullness of life for all.

2

Jewish and Christian Responses to Fear

I have already acknowledged how the writing of chapter 1 was influenced by world events. Indeed, so much of the daily news is so pertinent to our topic that I have been overwhelmed with material! Chapter 2, however, has been influenced by a different source: worship services during the Christian season of Advent. While I was writing these pages, I was also singing with my congregation:

Come, O long-expected Jesus,
born to set thy people free.
From our fears and sins release us;
let us find our rest in thee.

And on Christmas Eve, we heard again the great proclamation from the second chapter of Luke's Gospel: "The angel said to the shepherds, 'Do not be afraid; for see—I am bringing you good news of great joy for all the people.'" The point, as I heard it this Christmas Eve, is not that the angels were scary but that the calming of our fears is necessary in order to hear God's message of incarnate love.[1]

During this Advent season, there was also a funeral in the

congregation, a reminder that, most fundamentally, humans are anxious because we are finite. Our deepest longing for security can be traced to the fear of death. In the course of this particular funeral, we sang an eighteenth-century hymn known to most English-speaking Christians, "Amazing Grace," which includes the words "'twas grace that taught my heart to fear and grace my fears relieved." This means, I take it, that grace teaches us the fear of God, which, paradoxically, ensures that earthly fears, even the fear of dying, will not rule us. It is a fitting introduction to our discussion of how the Christian and Jewish traditions deal with the topic.

The Biblical Message

The Bible is not afraid of fear! Both the Hebrew Scriptures, authoritative for Judaism and Christianity, and the Christian New Testament speak often of fear, clearly acknowledging that it is a natural part of human life. Yet the message ringing throughout both testaments is unmistakable: "Be not afraid!" This is a frequent refrain in the accounts of Israel's early history: "Then Moses summoned Joshua and said to him, . . . 'It is the LORD who goes before you. He will be with you; he will not fail or forsake you. Do not fear or be dismayed'" (Deut. 31:8). We hear this from the prophets, especially Isaiah in the time of exile in Babylon: "Do not fear, for I am with you; do not be afraid, for I am your God" (Isa. 41:10) and "Do not fear, for I have redeemed you; I have called you by name, you are mine" (Isa. 43:1b). It is a major theme of the Psalms: "Even though I walk through the darkest valley [the valley of the shadow of death, KJV], I fear no evil; for you are with me" (Ps. 23:4) and "God is our refuge and strength, a very present help in trouble. Therefore we will not fear, though the earth should change, though the mountains shake in the heart of the sea" (Ps. 46:1–2). The part of my ordination service I remember most vividly is a sung rendition of Psalm 27: "The LORD is my light and my salvation; whom shall I fear? The LORD is the stronghold of my life; of whom shall I be afraid?" (Ps. 27:1). The theme is continued in the Christian Gospels: "Peace I leave with you; my peace I give to you. . . . Do not let your hearts be troubled, and do not let them be afraid" (John 14:27). "Do not be afraid": these, according to Scripture, are the words the angel Gabriel said to Mary (Luke 1:30) and Jesus said to Paul in a vision during the apostle's missionary journeys (Acts 18:9).

Seen through the lens of such texts (and there are many others), fear of earthly things is not simply a negative emotion; it is an expression of unbelief—a sign that one does not trust in God's redeeming, comforting, strengthening presence.

> Trust in the Lord, and do good; so you will live in the land, and enjoy security. (Ps. 37:3)

> In God, whose word I praise, in the Lord, whose word I praise, in God I trust; I am not afraid. What can a mere mortal do to me? (Ps. 56:10–11)

> Early in the morning [Jesus] came walking toward them on the sea. But when the disciples saw him walking on the sea, they were terrified, saying "It is a ghost!" And they cried out in fear. But immediately Jesus spoke to them and said, "Take heart, it is I; do not be afraid." Peter answered him, "Lord, if it is you, command me to come to you on the water." He said, "Come." So Peter got out of the boat, started walking on the water, and came toward Jesus. But when he noticed the strong wind, he became frightened, and beginning to sink, he cried out, "Lord, save me!" Jesus immediately reached out his hand and caught him, saying to him, "You of little faith, why did you doubt?" (Matt. 14:25–31)

This brings us back to the paradox noted above: The trust through which fear is overcome is often spoken of in these two biblical religions as "fear of the Lord." For example, Proverbs, a book in the Hebrew Scriptures, says that the fear of the Lord is "the beginning of wisdom" (Prov. 1:7 and 9:10), a "fountain of life" (Prov. 14:27) that enables those who have it to rest secure (Prov. 19:23). An even more paradigmatic passage is Deuteronomy 10:12: "So now, O Israel, what does the LORD your God require of you? Only to fear the LORD your God, to walk in all his ways, to love him, to serve the LORD your God with all your heart and with all your soul."

The Hebrew word here translated as "fear" is *yirah*, which can refer to the emotion we feel when confronted with danger, but it can also mean "awe" or "reverence." We do not fear God because God is cruel but because God is holy. Those who stand before the Creator do so with wonder—awe—at the glory and sanctity of the creation; from this stems a life of loving service, freed from fear. In this sense, fearing God is an ethical injunction, comparable to serving the Lord and walking in God's ways, of which the people must be reminded repeatedly.[2] Even fear of life's ending, which so often leads to destructive efforts at self-protection, is mitigated by trust in the Source of life itself.

When the Talmud, the ancient collection of rabbinic teachings and opinions, speaks of fear, it is almost exclusively the fear of God. We are told that Rabbi Akiva, a second-century leader of the Jewish people, held sessions on the Torah, even though it was forbidden by the Romans. When asked if he was afraid, he replied that we are commanded by the Holy One to study Torah all our days. If we are fearful when we do that, how much more fearful will we be should we cease to study its words?[3] Perhaps the best-known of the talmudic passages that touch on fear is a saying attributed to Rabbi Hanina: "Everything is in the hands of heaven [i.e., of God] except the fear [*yirah*] of heaven."[4] A contemporary rabbi, Toba Spitzer, interprets the meaning this way: "Everything is in the hands of a Reality that is beyond our control, except for our willingness to stand in awe of that Reality. . . . Our attitude can make the world a very small, constricted place or a place of wonder."[5] Fear of others is a symptom of constricted life; fear of God, however, is the basis of an appreciative life, a life that will not be bound by the fear that is so often evident in human society.

This is also the attitude found in the stories and aphorisms of the Hasidic masters collected by the famous Jewish scholar Martin Buber. For example: "Fear without love is something imperfect; love without fear is nothing at all."[6] In other words, without fear, what we love is not the holy and awesome Creator of all that is but only a small, convenient idol. And it leads to a faith that validates our fears and prejudices rather than challenging them. The esteemed teacher and talmudic scholar Joseph Soloveitchik was once asked why Jews should keep the prayer for *Yirat Adonai* (fear of the Lord) in the service for Yom Kippur. Because, he answered, "we pray that this great fear will free us from all lesser fears which lurk everywhere, upsetting and embittering our lives."[7] "Fear God" and "fear not others" are two sides of the same coin; both are commandments of Torah.

In my judgment, no one has written about this more powerfully than another well-known American rabbi, Abraham Joshua Heschel. A person, writes Heschel, can be motivated to do good works by a fear (*yirah*) of God's punishment, in this life and beyond; but, in the Jewish tradition, this is considered an inferior motivation.[8] Far more profound is responsive obedience to the sense of wonder and humility, the sense of awe (*yirah*) a person feels in the presence of the Holy Mystery we call God. Though the Hebrew word is the same, its two meanings are, in one sense, antithetical. "Awe, unlike fear, does not make us shrink from the awe-inspiring object, but, on the contrary, draws us near to it. This is why awe is compatible with both love and joy."[9] Awe, he writes elsewhere, "is more than an emotion; it is a way of understanding . . . an act of insight into a meaning greater than ourselves"[10]—which is why it is the beginning of wisdom.

I also love the insight of the long-time director of Harvard Hillel, Bernard Steinberg: "Awe is what happens to fear when it stops being about me."[11] Fear is a self-centered emotion: *I* am worried about that. *I* am afraid I can't possibly do that. Such fear dissipates when we look with reverence to God, not just ourselves.

Let's come at this from another direction. Scripture teaches that anxiety, which is what humans feel when we are insecure, follows from trusting in the wrong things to protect us. If, for example, our sense of worth and personal security is tied to the size of our bank account, then we will likely never have "enough."[12] This insight is succinctly illustrated in a parable found in the New Testament Gospel according to Luke. Jesus tells of a rich man who builds bigger barns to store his surfeit of stuff, so that he can "eat, drink, and be merry" without concern for others. But, of course, his abundance of earthly possessions cannot protect him from the fate of all humans (Luke 12:16–21). This is followed by a teaching on the futility of anxiety: "Can any of you by worrying [by fearing for the future] add a single hour to your span of life?"—or, as other translations have it, "add a cubit to your stature?" Rather, "do not be afraid, little flock," but trust in God and seek God's kingdom. Fear, as both Augustine and Thomas Aquinas observed, is born of love threatened. Loving the wrong things leads to needless fear—for "where your treasure it, there will your heart be also" (Luke 12:25, 32, 34).

I do not think it is a stretch to apply this teaching to nations. Can there be any doubt that the United States has amassed an abundance, a disproportionate share, of the world's resources? Or that we have become preoccupied with ways to protect what is "ours," to secure our way of life from outside threat? But, as Jesus teaches elsewhere in the Gospels, "no one can serve two masters. . . . You cannot serve God and wealth [Gk.: *mammon*]" (Matt. 6:24). If our choice is *mammon*, then we will need all the military power we can muster, all the walls we can build, to try to defend it. Indeed, security pursued through military force, seen through the lens of biblical religion, is the surest path to lasting insecurity—to perpetual fear. It is trusting in the wrong things.

Theological Approaches to Fear

It is striking how little the postbiblical Jewish tradition speaks of fear of anything other than God. We know that, tragically, many Jewish communities have lived in fear of persecution from their neighbors, especially in Christian-dominated regions; yet there are only infrequent references in Jewish literature to the need for courage in the face of human threats. One of these is from the Hasidic rabbi whose stories are regarded as the most "modern," Nahman of Bratslav. Rabbi Nahman taught that "the whole world is a narrow bridge. And the most important thing is not to be afraid"—an aphorism known to generations of Jews as a Hebrew folk song, "Kol Ha-Olam Kulo." He urged his followers to have "holy chutzpah," since determined courage, not fear, is needed to serve neighbor and God.[13]

Mention of the Hasidic tales is a reminder that storytelling has long been, in the Jewish tradition, a way of countering fear—including the exodus story ritually retold each year at Passover. There is a lot of fear at the beginning of the story, notes columnist David Brooks, which makes people apathetic and skeptical. He quotes the Torah scholar Avivah Zornberg, who says, "It is this fear that makes hearing, reverie, and speech impossible: a defensive rigidity that narrows the channels and closes the apertures." But, according to the commentaries, the Israelites told stories to one another, stories that opened up other possible worlds, until the people were strong enough to step out in freedom. "Storytelling," writes Brooks, "becomes central to conquering fear. It's a way of naming and making sense of fear and imagining different routes out. . . . Jews tell the story of the Exodus each generation to understand the fears they feel at that moment"[14]—and thus to live beyond them.

It is striking to me how much more attention has been paid to fear in the postbiblical Christian tradition. Prior to the modern period, the major Christian thinker who devoted most attention to the question of fear in human society (not simply the anxiety of standing before God) was Thomas Aquinas.[15] Drawing on the work of Aristotle and, to a lesser extent, Augustine, Aquinas understands fear as a "passion" or emotion that arises from the imagination of a future evil, from the threatened loss of something we love. In a world with no shortage of real dangers, fear is natural and necessary. Indeed, he writes, fearlessness is generally a vice, because it means we don't love anything enough to fear losing it. Fear has the potential to help shape the virtuous life by opening our eyes to loves we have taken for granted or forgotten. It can focus our attention and clarify our priorities.

The great "Doctor of the Church" also knows, however, that fear can, and often does, become toxic, constricting our vision and inhibiting our capacity for virtuous action. Fear should diminish, he writes, when a danger is remote. It follows that one indication a fear is "disordered" is when we are afraid of things that aren't imminently threatening. Residents of Guinea, Liberia, and Sierra Leone had reason to fear the Ebola virus in the fall of 2014; it was a contagious, life-threatening illness, already present in their West African communities, that had potentially awful consequences for themselves and their loved ones. But the Ebola scare in the United States, where the threat of infection was infinitesimal, was, by Aquinas's criteria, disordered, distracting attention from the compassionate response rightly demanded of Christians.

The problem is exacerbated in our era by the media that collapse distance, making even remote dangers seem immediate. Studies conducted by George Gerber, longtime dean of the Annenberg School for Communication at the University of Pennsylvania, found that television viewing is associated with a heightened sense of living in a "mean world" of violence and danger.[16] Television programming, from movies to the evening news, leads viewers to overestimate the rate of crime or the spread of disease or the prevalence of terrorism and increases their fear of becoming victims.

Aquinas's discussion of fear also invites readers to consider whether a perceived danger does in fact threaten the loss of something we love. Scott Bader-Saye, academic dean at Seminary of the Southwest, applies this question to the debate over same-sex marriage. Many persons in this country say they oppose gay unions because such unions threaten the integrity of "traditional marriage"—when there is little if any evidence to support such a fear and considerable reason to believe that the institution of marriage will be strengthened by allowing gay couples to live in sanctioned, covenantal relationship. "This is not to say," he writes, "that gay unions therefore should be blessed by the church—only that fear does not help us make a judgment about this issue."[17]

Then there is the matter of fearing the loss of things that shouldn't properly be loved. Many white persons seem to fear the loss of cultural, demographic preeminence. But isn't fear disordered if it is based on a love that excludes or diminishes others? Many Americans seem to fear the loss of a lifestyle built on an increasingly unsustainable use of natural resources. But is such a lifestyle worthy of our attachment if it threatens the well-being of our neighbors or of future generations?

Thomas Aquinas addresses this most directly in his discussion of "worldly love," that is, "the love whereby a man trusts in the world as his end."[18] Instead of looking to God for their security, humans often cling to possessions or money or power or status. Such accumulation of temporal things, in his judgment, only makes us more fearful, because we fear losing what we falsely love. Indeed, the more we have, the more we fear the loss of it.

Bader-Saye, in his helpful reading of Aquinas, points out that it is not always wrong to fear the loss of worldly possessions—which, while "goods of the least account," are still "goods." For example, he suggests, it is not wrong to fear the loss of one's home, but it is wrong to fear the loss of one's home so much that one limits one's practice of hospitality [an obvious virtue for Christians] to secure one's household. We might ask, then, whether gated communities represent a kind of disordered love in which the desire to protect the lesser good of one's property leads a person to reject the greater good of hospitality.[19]

Aquinas's discussion of fear is rooted in Scripture but also in the teaching of Aristotle, for whom the good person is one who fears "the right things, for the right motive, in the right manner, and at the right time."[20] The flip side of this is Aquinas's condemnation of the person who "fears what he ought not, and as he ought not."[21] We have already looked at fearing the wrong things (what we ought not fear). For Aquinas, fearing in the wrong way (as we ought not) seems to be when we fear so excessively that we allow the avoidance of evil to take precedence over the pursuit of good. At the individual level, we see this in persons whose fear of flying or crowds keeps them from visiting family or enjoying a concert, or whose excessive fear of crime restricts their participation in local community. But, from my perspective, we also see it at the corporate level when fear of crime inhibits programs aimed at the rehabilitation of offenders or legislation aimed at reducing the easy availability of guns.

Fear, writes the great theologian, implies a "contraction in the appetite"[22]—that is, a withdrawal into ourselves in order to fend off perceived danger. Yes, fear can be an expression of love. Too often, however, excessive fear curves people in on themselves, preventing them from living the virtuous life of welcome and generosity.

If this book were an exhaustive treatment of the subject, we would certainly turn now to other pre–twentieth century Christian thinkers—especially Søren Kierkegaard, whose book of 1844, *The Concept of Anxiety*, traced the universal experience of anxiety to the "dizzying" human freedom to choose good and evil, to choose what we will become. Kierkegaard anticipated twentieth-century discussions when he distinguished between fear and anxiety. A person is fearful over *something*; one is anxious, as it were, over *nothing*—over possibilities that have not yet come into being.[23]

I want to focus, however, on how, a century after Kierkegaard's reflections, "anxiety" became a widely used term in theology and culture, prompted in part by the increasing popularity of psychoanalysis and existentialist philosophy. The times were also conducive to the prevalence of this emotion. Arthur Schlesinger captured the public mood in his 1949 book *The Vital Center*: "Western man in the middle of the twentieth century is tense, uncertain, adrift. We look upon our epoch as a time of troubles, an age of anxiety. The grounds of our civilization, of our certitude, are breaking up under our feet, and familiar ideas and institutions vanish as we reach for them, like shadows in the failing dusk."[24]

In 1952, two major Christian thinkers—the Catholic theologian Hans Urs von Balthasar and the Protestant theologian/ philosopher Paul Tillich—published widely influential books aimed at addressing this "age of anxiety." The prescriptions offered by Balthasar, whose work is deeply scriptural and christocentric, and Tillich, who finds the source for "the courage to be" in "the God who transcends the God of the religions" are very different! Yet both may help us think about a religiously informed response to contemporary fear.

For Balthasar, author of *The Christian and Anxiety*, "the anxiety of modern man in a mechanized world where colossal machinery inexorably swallows up the frail human body and mind only to refashion it into a cog in the machinery"[25] is but one expression of finite humanity's ever-present anxiety. His argument, briefly stated, is that Christ has entered fully into the world's deep-seated anxiety in order to conquer it "completely and definitively." "Christ has borne the anxiety of the world so as to give to the world instead that which is his: his joy, his peace."[26] Although believers can always succumb anew to the powers and dominions, including anxiety, we can also leave fear behind to the extent that we appropriate in faith the truth of our redemption through the cross, to the extent we trust in God's life-giving grace embodied in the divine sacrifice of Jesus Christ. And once we, followers of Christ, are freed from human anxiety, we are freed as well to participate with joy in the "fruitful anguish" that comes from sharing in Christ's work of atonement, in his loving solidarity with anxious sinners. We can help take away the fears of the world.

Perhaps most importantly for our purposes, Balthasar wants to avoid both accommodation to the "greatly inflated" anxiety of the era and a "serene theology of irrelevance" that doesn't take such anxiety seriously. In his words, "[o]nly a Christian who does not allow himself to be infected by modern humanity's neurotic anxiety . . . has any hope of exercising a Christian influence on this age. He will not haughtily turn away from the anxiety of his fellow men and fellow Christians but will show them how to extricate themselves from their fruitless withdrawal into themselves and will point out the paths by which they can step out into the open, into faith's daring."[27]

Sixty-five years later, many Christians are more willing to grant that other religions also offer ways of overcoming fear. But Balthasar's basic challenge—to bring a religious message of hope to a fearful culture—surely remains timely and compelling.

Paul Tillich's *The Courage to Be*—despite its status as a theological bestseller, assigned in numerous seminary and university courses—is a complex book that eludes easy summary. For Tillich, anxiety is most basically the state in which a person is aware of her or his own mortality. But while this anxiety of death overshadows all others, it is important, writes Tillich, to distinguish two other types.

One of these, the anxiety of guilt or condemnation, comes from the judgment, often self-judgment, of our moral actions; it stems from the realization that what we have made of ourselves is unsatisfactory. This type of anxiety was dominant in Western history at the end of the medieval period—as seen, for example, in the anguished writings of Martin Luther.

It is the anxiety of meaninglessness, however, that, in Tillich's view, is most characteristic of our own era. It is experienced as emptiness, the loss of a spiritual center, the feeling that one has no place or purpose in a world that is, itself, without limits or coherence. Such anxiety—which Tillich sees expressed by such modern writers as Kafka, Eliot, Sartre, and Arthur Miller, as well as by various artists—causes many of our contemporaries to flock to new forms of collectivist authority. These include Nazism, communism, and what he calls "democratic conformism"—participation in the "big machine of production and consumption." While not suggesting that these are morally equivalent, Tillich does suggest that, in each, courage is gained, and the anxiety of meaninglessness is reduced, through involvement in the group and its collective values.[28] This modern type of anxiety has also led people, as the American experience certainly attests, to seek absolute answers from religion, clinging to an authoritarian tradition or an inerrant Bible. Fanaticism, Tillich argues, "shows the anxiety which it was supposed to conquer, by attacking with disproportionate violence those who disagree and who demonstrate by their disagreement elements in the spiritual life of the fanatic which he must suppress in himself. Because he must suppress them in himself he must suppress them in others. His anxiety forces him to persecute dissenters."[29] Believers try to reduce the anxiety of creeping meaninglessness by defending "the castle of undoubted certitude," which, however, "is not built on the rock of reality."[30]

Tillich contends that the anxiety that is potentially present in every individual becomes general and acute when "the accustomed structures of meaning, power, belief, and order disintegrate"[31]—which tends to happen at the end of an era, a time of great social transformation. Structures and assumptions that have functioned to keep anxiety at bay no longer work, leading to what we now call culture wars. "Conflicts between the old, which tries to maintain itself, often with new means, and the new, which deprives the old of its intrinsic power, produce anxiety in all directions."[32] Some speak of their fear of being confined within outdated patterns and teachings (e.g., old understandings of marriage that justify resistance to the rights of same-sex couples), others their fear of change that seems to have no clear direction or center (e.g., the unprecedented acceptance of same-sex marriage that ignores tradition).

Another part of Tillich's argument, drawn from depth psychology and existentialist philosophy (including Kierkegaard), is the distinction between anxiety and fear. Fear, as we noted in the introduction, has a definite object, which we can identify and to which we can respond. Anxiety leaves us with a feeling of helplessness; thus "anxiety strives toward fear," because "fear can be met by courage."[33] Bader-Saye helps make this more concrete:

> Just as we long for a diagnosis when we are sick, so we long for a way to name and locate our chaotic fears. Once we have a diagnosis, we know how to respond to our illness. We feel that we can *do* something. Likewise, once we locate an object [or person] for our fear, we feel empowered. We can now take tangible steps to make ourselves more safe. Insecurity is no longer the sad reality of a fallen and vulnerable world; it is the result of "those" people who pose a tangible and definable threat to "us" and our way of life. Indeed, we exist as "us" precisely because we oppose what "they" are and what "they" do.[34]

It is not hard to apply this analysis to mid-twentieth-century America. The previous three generations had experienced truly mind-boggling transition: from horses and trains to automobiles and air travel; from candles to electricity; from a predominantly agrarian society to cites of the industrial revolution; from mail and telegraph to radio and television; from fairly rudimentary medical care to x-rays, penicillin, and vaccines; and in warfare, from rifles to atomic bombs. Not to mention two world wars and an assault on teachings long taken for granted by traditional religious believers. When Auden wrote about "the age of anxiety," the title felt apt, without even the need for explanation. So it is not surprising that the country witnessed a surge in nationalist fervor and, for the most part, "welcomed" the fear of communism and the U.S.S.R. (a fear that, in the eyes of most historians, was often expressed in ways unwarranted by the actual threat). It gave an outlet for pent-up anxiety, provided a focus for our fear to which we could respond—just as targeting Muslims or refugees gives focus to contemporary anxiety.

For Tillich, the proper response to anxiety, including the modern epidemic of it, is "courage," understood as the strength to affirm one's life "in spite of" guilt, meaninglessness, and the inevitability of one's own death. The anxiety that is part of life leads to an understandable striving for security. But no final security is possible; and the search for it becomes pathological when we fear "what is not to be feared," imprisoning ourselves by our misplaced apprehensions.[35]

This analysis of the human condition has proved valuable for Christians for more than half a century. Perhaps less compelling, though certainly provocative, is Tillich's assertion that the God of traditional theism cannot be the source of this "courage to be." If God is a Being, even though greater than all other beings, then God is still, in some sense, finite and cannot help allay the anxiety inherent in our finitude. Only a "God above God"—God understood as the ground of being itself—can sustain the courage to affirm life in spite of a chaotic world and a finite existence.[36]

Easier to endorse, perhaps, is Tillich's insistence that Christian theologians "should decide for truth against safety, even if the safety is consecrated and supported by the churches."[37] Christians, in other words, should not be afraid to face head-on the sources of human anxiety and should resist schemes of security that pit us against others or thwart the development of courage "in spite of."

The final Christian text I want to examine, titled *In Search of Security*, is written not by an individual scholar but by a task force of bishops from the United Methodist Church, and it is approved by the entire UMC Council of Bishops for use in congregations. The document is of special interest because it was produced in the immediate aftermath of the attacks on September 11, 2001, and focuses on a dominant word in contemporary American society: "security."

Drawing on Scripture, the bishops begin by stressing that security is a basic human need; it was, for example, a central aspect of the salvation God offered to Israel (see, e.g., Deut. 12:10; 33:12, 28). In biblical perspective, however, security is a function not of power but of trust in God. They point out that the Hebrew word *batach* means both "to trust" and "to be secure." It refers to the safety humans feel when we rely, through faithful obedience, not on our righteousness or our strength but on the One whose creative will fashioned all that is (Isa. 31:1–3).[38]

In the New Testament, according to the bishops, human security is even less of an issue; indeed, "following Jesus leads to radical insecurity."[39] They quote social ethicist Theodore Weber: "If the resurrection is truth, then whatever true security might mean, it is to be found on the other side of exposure to suffering and death."[40] It is to be found in the conviction "that neither death, nor life, nor angels, nor rulers, nor things present, nor things to come, nor powers, nor height, nor depth, nor anything else in all creation, will be able to separate us from the love of God in Christ Jesus our Lord" (Rom. 8:38–39). Christians should not expect total security in this world. The very desire for it points us in the wrong direction, since Christian faith both calls us to vulnerable service on behalf of others and assures us of God's abiding presence—even in the valley of the shadow of death. The bishops obviously agree with Marilynne Robinson that "fear is not a Christian habit of mind."[41]

The most helpful section of the document, in my judgment, comes when the bishops put these biblical teachings in dialogue with our experience of living in a world of real and at times immediate dangers. They acknowledge the need for police to maintain law and order; they say, through gritted teeth, that military action may be needed, as a last resort, when vulnerable people are under assault. None of this, however, brings genuinely long-term security for society as a whole. Furthermore, when we respond to a challenge out of fear, we often make the situation worse. It was in an atmosphere of fear that the United States prosecuted a war in Iraq that ultimately strengthened terrorists rather than destroying them. Fear led the United States to squander on war resources that could have been used to promote development and justice. Fear has led this country to weaken the very freedoms we ostensibly are defending militarily. "As Christian people," the bishops declare, "we share the anxiety and the fears of the people around us. But we know the One who did not cease to tell his disciples: Do not be afraid. Therefore, our contribution to the process of decision-making in our society should be to avoid fear-driven overreactions to the challenges we face and to work for solutions that solve the problems in a constructive way."[42]

As a kind of summation, the Methodist bishops draw on the work of the Franciscan theologian Bryan Massingale, from whom we heard in chapter 1. Father Massingale argues that American society is faced with "two competing visions of security, rooted in two highly divergent world views. The first, rooted in a world of fear, seeks security in military power directed to the end of defending economic privilege for a few. The other, rooted in a world view of blessing, sees security lying in the effort of assuring that the blessings of creation are enjoyed by all."[43]

While this typology is surely too simplistic (e.g., not all people who champion security through military strength do so simply to protect economic privilege), it is a reminder that the Christian message differs radically from the ethos of US society. It also points to a central New Testament claim: Christians are called to live vulnerably as participants in God's risky mission of serving those in need and reconciling those who are estranged. To borrow a formulation from the Russian Christian philosopher Nikolai Berdyaev, security for oneself is a *material* issue—not necessarily sinful, but also not a highest value. Security for one's neighbor, however, is a *spiritual* issue. Protecting persons who are most at risk, even when it is risky, is the calling of those who follow Jesus.

This is, at least for me, very difficult territory. I profess to be a Christian, and yet the gospel's radical challenge to our fear-based culture often frightens me! I give thanks for the security that comes from having a decent pension, ample possessions, a good cardiologist, and responsive local police. Is it possible, without renouncing such things, to take seriously the Christian teaching that true security comes from giving away, not possessing? Can I appreciate the freedom from fear I have and at the same time try to live in such a way that I help alleviate the anxiety felt by others? At the national level, can I give thanks for those who protect this country from attack, while also resisting what Furedi calls "the worship of safety,"[44] which exaggerates threats and turns suspicion into a virtue?

Human Interdependence

I will end this chapter on the Jewish and Christian responses to fear by turning to a public figure admired by Jews and Christians alike, Dr. Martin Luther King Jr. King spoke often about fear, focusing on it directly in at least two published sermons, "Antidotes for Fear" (1957) and "The Mastery of Fear" (1962). The whole system of racial segregation, he points out, was buttressed by irrational fears: "fear of losing a preferred economic position, fear of losing social status, fear of intermarriage, fear of adjusting to a new situation."[45] But King also insists that fear is characteristic of modern life as a whole, leaving a great many people "psychologically wrecked and spiritually dejected."[46]

How are we to address this widespread and deep-seated problem? King's answer is suggested by his scriptural text for both sermons: "There is no fear in love, but perfect love casts out fear" (1 John 4:18). Bigger armaments will not cast out fear; they exacerbate it. More possessions will not cast out fear; they increase it. The only antidote is the assurance that we are loved by a God who sends us to love even those sick with "the poisonous disease of fear."[47] King would certainly agree with Marilyn McEntyre that the security God offers is not a promise of what won't happen (e.g., no terrorist attacks) but a promise of what will happen: that God will be with us even in the midst of life-threatening danger.[48]

In my judgment, however, Dr. King's greatest contribution to this topic is his eloquent insistence on recognizing the reality of human interdependence. Americans of any and no religion may well know these words from his "Christmas Sermon on Peace": "We are all caught in an inescapable network of mutuality, tied in a single garment of destiny. Whatever affects one directly affects all indirectly."[49] Such interdependence, which Christianity and Judaism ground theologically in the conviction that life comes from a single Creator, means that true security can never be achieved through unilateral defense but, rather, through attentiveness to the injustice, the anxiety, that afflicts other children of God. Former archbishop of Canterbury Rowan Williams puts it succinctly: "There is no security apart from common security." South Korea will be insecure so long as North Korea feels threatened. Israel "will have security only when Palestinians have hope."[50] European security, as recent events have shown, is intertwined with that of North Africa and the Middle East. US security depends, among other things, on reducing the economic disparities that fuel global resentment.

It is not surprising that a fearful nation spends nearly twenty times as much on its military as it does on foreign economic assistance.[51] But this fact should at least raise questions for people of religious faith: Isn't true, long-lasting security more a matter of schools and clinics than of guns and bombs? Shouldn't the children who died of hunger or disease on 9/11 be as important to us as those who died in the terrorist attacks?[52] Won't God hold us accountable for the way we respond to the anxieties of our global neighbors? Has fear caused us to make an idol of "defense"?

3

The Response of Other Religions to Fear

In the fall of 2015, I had the pleasure of attending the sixth gathering of the Parliament of the World's Religions, which met in Salt Lake City, Utah. In addition to exciting plenary sessions, there were hundreds of workshops and seminars, each one described in some detail in a thick conference guidebook. As I read through this cornucopia of offerings, however, I was struck by the fact that not a single one dealt, at least directly, with the topic of fear.

The book you are now reading cannot fully remedy that omission, since my academic training is in Christian theology, not in the history and thought (and languages!) of other religions. No matter how much I read or how many interviews I conduct, I cannot have a believer's perspective on religions other than Christianity. I can, however, point toward the perhaps-surprising prevalence of this theme in the sacred writings of other faith traditions. While noting obvious differences in the way various religions understand fear, I can also point toward broad commonalities—commonalities that I hope will provide a basis for shared interfaith witness.

As we have already seen, fear of God—and, therefore, not

of humans—is an important concept in religions that have their roots in the Middle East. The Bahá'í faith, a monotheistic religion founded by a "divine Messenger" called Bahá'u'lláh in nineteenth-century Persia (modern Iran), is another case in point. There are dozens of passages in the Bahá'í sacred texts urging adherents to "let God be your fear," to be adorned "with the ornament of the fear of God."[1] According to Bahá'u'lláh, such fear is "the fountainhead of all goodly deeds and virtues"[2]—a point that is expanded by Shoghi Effendi, the Messenger's great-grandson and definitive interpreter in the twentieth century: "Only a relatively highly evolved soul would always be disciplined by love alone. Fear of punishment, fear of the anger of God if we do evil, is needed to keep people's feet on the right path."[3] Most important, of course, is to love God; but it is the love for a divine Parent who is both merciful and just.

The flip side of this teaching is that reliance on God is the key to eliminating fear in everyday life. "Those who place their whole trust in God," writes Dale Lehman, a contemporary Bahá'í commentator, "need fear nothing but God, for His will cannot be thwarted. . . . The love of God; trust in God; reliance upon God. Those who have these treasures have everything and need fear nothing."[4] Indeed, fear is incompatible with these "treasures," for, in the words of the Bahá'u'lláh, "love is a light that never dwells in a heart possessed by fear."[5]

Despite the significant differences between Western and Eastern religions, similar ideas are found in religions stemming from the Indian subcontinent. For example, Guru Nanak Dev, founder of the Sikh religion, taught that humans, if they are to experience God—if, to use terminology typical of Sikhism, they are to lose the egocentric self in the Universal Being—should cultivate two qualities in their daily lives: to live without animosity and to live without fear.[6]

How can a person live fearlessly? The simple answer—set forth in the Sikh holy book, the Guru Granth Sahib—will sound familiar: "One who does not fear God shall live in fear."

"Without the fear of God, how can anyone become fearless?"[7] When a person begins to fear God only, to focus through meditation and selfless service on the one Creator, rather than on the self and its attachment to worldly values, all other fears can be mastered. A Sikh "overcomes all fear by cherishing [the word can also be translated "fearing"] the Fearless Lord."[8] A recent article by the Sikh Missionary Society in the United Kingdom applies this religious wisdom to terrorism of all kinds: "In Guru Nanak's teachings, none who spread fear and insecurity are spared: the king and his henchmen using terror as an administrative tool; the high caste priest using rituals, superstition and social divisions as his devices for exploitation; the corrupt religious judge selling judgments; and the religious fanatic seeking converts to his own faith through force."[9] A Sikh, they conclude, can stand without fear before those who spread fear, knowing that terror will not prevail in God's creation. All of this is beautifully summarized in what may be the prime injunction of the Sikh religion: Fear no one and make no one afraid.[10]

Fear and Islam

We might expect some similarity between the Bahá'í and Sikh religions, since both have been influenced, to some extent, by Islam. But what about religious traditions nurtured in very different cultural soils and historical contexts? With this question in mind, I want to look in greater depth at Islam and Buddhism. What do these very dissimilar religions have to say about fear? Are there common themes that emerge even out of substantially different worldviews?

In one sense, the Islamic understanding of fear is an easy topic: when Muslim scholars speak of fear, it is almost always fear of God [in Arabic, Allah] and of God's promised day of judgment. These teachings are primarily grounded in the Qur'an, the sacred text for Muslims, and, secondarily, in the Hadith, a collection of traditions containing sayings attributed to the Prophet Muhammad. I want to begin, however, by pointing to a book by the most important thinker in medieval Islam, Abu Hamid Muhammed al-Ghazali. Al-Ghazali, whose work is repeatedly cited by Thomas Aquinas, contributed greatly to the renewal of Islam through his four-volume masterpiece *The Revival of the Religious Sciences.* The fourth volume deals with the means of salvation—that is, the "cure" of souls—and one section is titled "The Book of Fear and Hope." Although written at the end of the eleventh century, it remains the most influential discussion of fear in non-Qur'anic Muslim literature.

In the introduction to his translation of "The Book of Fear and Hope," William McKane argues that al-Ghazali is "a kind of medical officer of [spiritual] health" who regards fear and hope as complementary "therapies," prescribed in the Qur'an ("call upon Him in fear and in hope" [7:56]), for restoring proper balance to the soul.[11] To alter the metaphor, fear is commendable, writes al-Ghazali, because it is "the whip of God by which he drives his creatures towards perseverance in knowledge and action, so that by means of both of these they may obtain the rank of nearness to God."[12] Such fear may come from knowledge of God and God's awesome power or from knowledge of our sinfulness; but, whatever its cause, it can stimulate obedience to the divinely given ethical precepts of Islam.

This does not mean, however, that all fear is good or that more fear is better than less. According to al-Ghazali, fear can be "deficient" if it results only in momentary feeling, not in active, long-term obedience to God's will. And it can be "extreme" if it leads to despair, which also stultifies action. Thus fear and hope should exist in equilibrium in the life of a believer.[13] This idea is captured in a quotation from Ali, the cousin and son-in-law of the Prophet and a key leader in the early history of Islam: "The knowledgeable person is simply he who does not make people despair of the mercy of God [i.e., lose hope] and does not make them feel secure from the stratagems of God [i.e., lose fear]."[14]

Throughout the book, al-Ghazali rails against false, worldly forms of security, because they turn people from the commendable fear of God. Those who seek security in this world are "arrogant and ignorant and remiss."[15] Their souls, writes the spiritual doctor, are not in proper balance.

We hear echoes of al-Ghazali's argument in the work of another prominent medieval scholar and jurist, Ibn Qayyim al-Jawziyyah. Ibn Qayyim was an interpreter of the Sufi tradition, which speaks of the various "stations" (stages) that a soul must master in the search for intimacy with God. One of these, he wrote in his classic treatise on spirituality, is the "station of fear," which is "most beneficial for the heart" and "an obligation on everyone"[16]—but needs proper balance. "The heart in its journey towards Allah is like a bird whose head is love, and hope and fear are its two wings." If either wing is damaged, the bird cannot fly; but at any given moment one wing or the other may appropriately receive more attention. During good times, when the community may be tempted to rely less on God, leaders should strengthen the wing of fear. When the community faces danger or a person faces death, leaders should strengthen the wing of hope.[17]

There is no discussion in either "The Book of Fear and Hope" or "The Station of Fear" of fearing persons and things other than God. This question *is* addressed, however, by Islamic scholars who build on al-Ghazali's foundation. A good example, available in English, is found in *Ethics and Spiritual Growth*, by the contemporary Iranian cleric Sayyid Mujtaba Musavi Lari. Lari shows the influence of al-Ghazali when he contends that "in human nature, hope and fear have been put together."[18] As a result, the virtue of courage lies midway between the extremes of "excess and neglect"—that is, too much fear (which forgets hope), and too little fear (which overemphasizes hope). God has infinite compassion; but a person who pins all her hopes on God's forgiveness and mercy, without trepidation concerning the consequences of her conduct, will likely succumb to the human tendency toward selfish, immoral behavior.

But this principle of balancing fear and hope, taught across the centuries, also has another benefit: It "relieves the human being from every kind of fear which oppresses the soul and which has no bearing on real life."[19] God alone has the power of life and death, so why fear mundane, transitory forces? God alone has the power to cause harm or benefit, so why fear other persons (a sentiment reminiscent of the Psalms)? "That which should be feared," writes Lari, "is that Power that embraces every being in its omnipotence, sovereignty, and dispensation. It is that which grants and deprives, gives and takes away."[20]

Beyond this, when fear in everyday life, fear of things other than God, dominates a person's life, it does not allow for the development of courage—a key theme for Lari and other Muslim scholars. Without courage, he suggests, we easily bow to common prejudices, succumb to trends that promote ostentation, acquiesce to the mob's call for vengeance. This much is certain: "[O]ne cannot succeed in overcoming life's hardships through fear and anxiety. . . . One whose thoughts are constantly assailed by fear and panic will find the world grim and horrifying."[21]

Thus it is vain to trust in other powers for protection. The Qur'an expresses this in a famous parable. Those who take protectors apart from God have a house like that of a spider (29:41), easily torn asunder by the elements or passing animals. (Christians will be reminded of a house built on sand [Matt. 7:24–27].) Fear in human life can even be called sinful if it betrays a lack of trust in God and hinders us from fulfilling our God-given duty to love our neighbors, even those who may seem scary—an idea we encountered in Aquinas.

There are as many as a dozen words in the Qur'an that carry the meaning of the English word "fear." For example, in sura (chapter) 3, verse 175 ("So fear them [the people gathered against you] not, but fear Me, if you are believers"), the Arabic word used is *khawf*, which is fear of physical danger from which one flees. However, in 5:44 ("So fear not mankind, but fear Me") the word is *khashya*, which is fear associated with knowledge of God.[22] To know the greatness of God is to stand before God in reverence and awe. A person who experiences such awe, such fear, does not flee *from* its Source, but *to* it.

I mention this, not only because it indicates real similarity with the Christian and Jewish understanding, but because it helps give proper nuance to the "fear of God" in Islam. American Muslim leaders with whom I have spoken about this topic emphasize that, in the final analysis, faith in God is based on love, not fear. To quote again from Ali, "My Lord, I do not worship you out of fear of your punishment, nor out of hope for your reward; I worship you because I have found you worthy of worship."[23] As one Muslim colleague put it to me, "faithfulness stems from love of God, but ethical behavior needs the additional motivation of fear." The two go hand in hand. Every command named in the Qur'an, no matter how apparently alarming or burdensome, originates in the divine mercy of One who cares for us with chastisement as well as comfort.

My conversation partners also insist that everyday human fear is a natural part of life, an idea supported in the sacred texts. According to the Qur'an, Moses, after he mistakenly killed an Egyptian, was afraid of Pharaoh. Abraham felt fear when his angelic visitors would not eat what he had prepared.[24] In various hadiths, we read of the struggles of the early Muslim community, including their fear in the face of powerful opponents, and even of the Prophet Muhammad's fears of failing to fulfill his mission on earth.[25] It follows that the fear felt by refugees or persecuted minorities or those caught in the midst of violence is natural and understandable and should be responded to with empathy rather than disapproval.

This point is particularly important, given the fear felt today by many Muslims living in the United States. The most recent edition of the annual report on Islamophobia, published by the Council on American-Islamic Relations (aptly titled *Confronting Fear*), indicates that in 2015 there were seventy-eight incidents in which mosques were the targets of attack or vandalism. Anti-Islam bills have now become law in ten states, a sign of the legally sanctioned animosity, driven by fear, that is making Muslims understandably afraid.[26] One young Muslim woman, following an intimidating verbal assault, told a journalist, "I am terrified. My friends are scared. My family is scared. I'm scared for other people."[27]

The imams with whom I spoke emphasized that such fear deserves what Christians would call a "pastoral" response. But in their sermons they continue to discourage fear of anything other than God's displeasure. After all, Muslim communities experience daily the detrimental effects that fear has on societies! And, in the final analysis, there is no need for it, since "whosoever follows my guidance, no fear shall come upon them, nor shall they grieve" (2:38).

Fear and Buddhism

Let me make explicit what is probably evident to most readers: It is always risky to speak about *the* Christian or *the* Jewish or *the* Muslim understanding of a topic such as fear. Theological differences between Catholic and Protestant Christians, Orthodox and Reform Jews, Sunni and Shiite Muslims mean that general statements will always need caveats.

This may be even more true of Buddhism, which is marked by significant differences among its various schools. Even so basic a question as "Is Buddhism a theistic religion?" will elicit disparate—or at least disparately nuanced—responses. My opening observations on the Buddhist understanding of fear draw heavily on readings from and conversations with scholars who identify with Theravada Buddhism. After that, however, I will review two recent books by scholars in the Mahayana tradition, with the hope that through this approach I will accurately express ideas affirmed by most persons who seek to follow the teachings of Gautama Buddha.

Buddhist scholars, consistent with what we have seen in other religious traditions, often note that fear, which is a natural and pervasive part of life, can be either healthy or unhealthy— to use Buddhist terminology, "skillful" or "unskillful." Fear is unskillful when we are afraid of things that are unlikely to harm us or occurrences that are inevitable—most notably, separation and death. Such fears lead people to grasp for illusory forms of security and thus contribute to unhappiness and suffering. Skillful fear, by contrast, motivates us to take constructive steps in the face of danger. Indeed, it is the fear of suffering that can move us to take control of our minds through meditation, which is the only way out of the cycle of fear and suffering.

To come at this from another direction, Buddhism understands human fear to be rooted in distorted ways of looking at ourselves and the world. There is disagreement within Buddhism over whether perceived reality is literally "real," but there is broad agreement that the world does not exist separately from the mind. Much of what we perceive as fearful is actually a projection of our own consciousness. In the words of Shantideva, a famous eighth-century monk, the Buddha teaches that "all fears and all infinite sufferings arise from the mind. . . . [I]t is not possible to control all external events; but if I simply control my mind, what need is there to control other things?"[28]

Because of confusion (what Buddhist texts often call "delusion") in our minds, we fear losing things—for example, wealth, family, or power—to which we are attached, attachments that are inevitably frustrated by the world's impermanence. This is poetically expressed in a passage from the Dhammapada, a collection of sayings from the Buddha that is one of the most widely read Buddhist scriptures:

> From what is dear, grief is born,
> from what is dear, fear is born.
> For someone freed from what is dear,
> there is no grief—
> so why fear?
> . . . .
> From craving, grief is born,
> from craving, fear is born.
> For someone freed from craving,

there is no grief—
so why fear?[29]

Even hope, which in Western religions is the positive balance
to fear, is seen in Buddhism as a source of attachment. For
someone freed from hope, there is no grief—so why fear?
The way out of the cycle of fear, in Buddhist teaching, is
to look deeply at our fear (which, in a sense, is what I hope to
encourage with this book). By becoming aware of our fears—
confronting them, thinking deeply about them—we can recognize that fear often leads us to see danger where there is little
or none. "If we obsess over non-existent or trivial dangers,"
writes the American monk Thanissaro Bhikkhu, a follower
of the Thai forest tradition, "we'll squander time and energy
building useless defenses, diverting our attention from genuine threats."[30] Meditation on our fear also helps us see how our
attachments often cause us to act in ways that harm others and
ourselves—and that in the final analysis cannot protect us.

Contrary to popular stereotypes, Buddhism is not compla-
cent with regard to possible harm—quite the opposite. Com-
placency, not facing the real source of our fears, means that we
react to them with confusion, often in ways that create fear in
others. It is only when we become "heedful" of the nature of
our fears that we can overcome them.

One writer who develops these themes with an American
audience in mind is the Buddhist nun Pema Chödrön, a US-
born disciple of Tibetan masters. In books such as *The Places
That Scare You: A Guide to Fearlessness in Difficult Times*,
Chödrön contends that human beings "put up protective walls
made of opinions, prejudices, and strategies, barriers that
are built on a deep fear of being hurt."[31] Drawing on teaching from the Mahayana Buddhist tradition, she focuses on
three strategies people use to give the illusion of security: (a)
we fill the space around us with things or activities that make
us feel protected; (b) we fill our minds with beliefs or ideolo-
gies that give the illusion of certainty; (c) we fill our time with

experiences—sports, drugs, even spiritual practices—that mask the world's impermanence.[32] In short, humans look for security and happiness in all the wrong places (a familiar theme!), resisting the irrefutable truth of aging and death, which only increases our fear and suffering.

Buddhist teachings, as Chödrön puts it, "encourage us to relax gradually and wholeheartedly into the ordinary and obvious truth of change."[33] The meditative practice of mindfulness, on which she elaborates in this and other writings, enables its practitioners to face life without self-delusions, to go "to places that scare you." It is a method for affirming ourselves unconditionally but also for overcoming the mental and emotional distance that promotes indifference to the sufferings of others. Indeed, mindfulness training helps us to recognize the fundamental interconnectedness of life, "to grow in understanding that when we harm another, we are harming ourselves."[34] Our fear, the root of anger and aggression, can make other persons afraid—which, unless we break the cycle, can contribute to our anxiety.

Training in *bodhichitta*—that is, spiritual practices aimed at attaining an "enlightened mind," a mind and heart completely open to the pain we share with other beings—offers no promise, she cautions, of happy endings, no easy avoidance of fear. "Rather, this 'I' who wants to find security—who wants something to hold on to—can finally learn to grow up."[35] By getting to know our fears, we find that they lose their hold on our lives.

These ideas are reinforced in the highly popular work of the Vietnamese Zen master Thich Nhat Hanh, whose more than forty books in English include the 2012 publication *Fear: Essential Wisdom for Getting through the Storm*. According to Nhat Hanh, "nonfear is the cream of the Buddha's teaching," because "fear spoils our lives and makes us miserable."[36] The primary fear is, of course, the fear of death—which, he teaches, stems from our misperception of true reality. Ocean waves serve as a useful image. We perceive each wave as having a beginning and an end. We think we can compare waves, one being more beautiful or more powerful than another. When we look in depth, however, we see that waves are, in truth, nothing more (or less) than water. Individual waves are part of a far greater whole, a whole characterized by constant ebb and flow, in which beginning and end, better and worse, have no meaning. The same, he writes, is true of human life. We perceive ourselves as beginning to be at a certain moment in time and ceasing to be at another; but this is to miss the ultimate reality of which our lives are a part. Once we recognize that birth and death are simply concepts, not the way things are, we lose the fear that is the basis of our vain craving. Like a cloud that becomes rain that evaporates to form clouds, nothing is born and nothing dies, but all is part of an ever-changing cosmos. Grasping this insight frees us from the illusion of securing ourselves from change, and thus frees us from fear.[37]

How do we escape from our illusions? Here Nhat Hanh echoes Chödrön and other Buddhist teachers: "Only by looking deeply into the nature of your fear can you find the way out."[38] It is the practice of living fully in the present moment—mindfulness—that gives us the courage to face our fears. Said the Buddha, "The past no longer is, the future is not yet here; there is only one moment in which life is available, and that is the present moment."[39] This doesn't preclude making plans; but it means there is no use being afraid about the future. It doesn't forbid remembering the past; but it means there is no use living in sorrow and fear because of what has been.

As all of this indicates, Buddhism generally focuses more on the individual than on society. Social change, Buddhists assume, begins with the training of the mind of each adherent. This still means, however, that Buddhist practice has social implications, and Thich Nhat Hanh makes some of these explicit. When people act out of fear, he teaches, they affect each other, eventually creating a "culture of fear" in which the society, like the individuals in it, grasps at illusory forms of security. If military might were an antidote to the fear of terrorism, he points out, then the United States would not be consumed by anxiety.[40]

Nations, like individuals, do not like feeling afraid; so fear often turns to anger, even hatred. Someone must pay for making us afraid! Instead of seeking to understand the roots of terrorist activity, instead of promoting our own safety by working to help others feel safe in this interdependent world, we react to it as a nation with vengeance—reinforcing the cycle of fear and violence. Thanissaro Bhikkhu (bhikkhu being the Pali language word for "monk") writes of this same dynamic, noting that individually and corporately "we react to genuine dangers in ways that, instead of ending the dangers, actually create new ones."[41] For example, weapons, aimed at stopping terrorists, incite a resentment that breeds further terrorism: "The most unskillful response to fear is when, perceiving dangers to our own life or property, we believe we can gain strength and security by destroying the lives and property of others. The delusion pervading our fear makes us lose perspective. If other people were to act this way, we would know they were wrong. But somehow, when we feel threatened, our standards change, our perspective warps, so that wrong seems right as long as *we're* the ones doing it."[42]

Of course, it finally comes back to our individual selves. We may not be persons who blow up planes and markets, but we are persons who harbor the same emotions as those who do, persons who can "terrorize" others with our behavior. What is needed, writes Nhat Hanh, is a community of practitioners "generating a collective energy of mindfulness" in order to begin to change our culture of fear.[43]

One political leader who seems to have been shaped by such teachings is Myanmar's Aung San Suu Kyi. In a famous speech, "Freedom from Fear," delivered in 1990 and subsequently published in a book by the same title, Suu Kyi argued that "it is not power that corrupts but fear"—both the fear felt by those who wield power and the fear felt by those who are subject to it. "With so close a relationship between fear and corruption, it is little wonder that in any society where fear is rife corruption in all forms becomes deeply entrenched."[44]

Part of the speech lifts up the memory of her father, the revolutionary leader Aung San, who exhorted the Burmese people to develop courage. She applied to him words once used by Nehru to describe Gandhi: "The essence of his teaching was fearlessness and truth." Nehru, Suu Kyi reminded her audience, was a political modernist; but in assessing the needs of his new nation, he drew on the religious heritage of ancient India: "The greatest gift for an individual or a nation . . . [is] *abhaya*, fearlessness, not merely bodily courage but absence of fear from the mind."[45] The revolution needed in Myanmar, she declared, is a "revolution of the spirit." Among the freedoms to which this revolution should aspire, "freedom from fear stands out both as a means and an end. A people who would build a nation in which strong, democratic institutions are firmly established as a guarantee against state-induced power must first learn to liberate their own minds from apathy and fear."[46] Her political message is unmistakable, but so is the influence of her Buddhist heritage.

A Concluding Word on Hinduism

I will end this chapter with a brief look at the world religion not yet discussed: Hinduism. I do so with trepidation, since, in the eyes of many scholars, "Hinduism is nothing more than a generic term for a family of diverse religious tendencies,"[47] all of which accept the authority of ancient Sanskrit scriptures known as the Vedas. With this diversity in mind, I have decided to focus our attention on the work of one man, Swami Vivekananda, a central figure in the late-nineteenth- and early-twentieth-century movement for the renaissance of this hard-to-pin-down religion.

It was clear to educated Indians of the era that the people of the subcontinent, while possessing a rich and ancient culture, had suffered great degradation—socially, morally, and religiously—during the period of British colonization. One response was "Hindu Modernism," also called "Neo-Vedanta" (Vedanta being a prominent stream of Indian philosophy), a movement that sought to recover and reinterpret the teachings of classical Hinduism in conversation with Western ideas. Vivekananda was pivotal in this effort, having been inspired by the nineteenth-century Bengali mystic Sri Ramakrishna, and serving in turn as inspiration for younger leaders, including Rabindranath Tagore, Sarvapalli Radhakrishnan, and Mahatma Gandhi. Vivekananda's address to the Parliament of the World's Religions in 1893 (the first in this series), along with the Ramakrishna Mission that he founded in 1897, has also been highly influential for the Western perception of Hinduism.

The rejection of fear is at the core of Vivekananda's teaching:

The whole secret of existence is to have no fear.[48]

Fear is death, fear is sin, fear is hell, fear is unrighteousness, fear is wrong life. All the negative thoughts and ideas that are in this world have proceeded from this evil spirit of fear.[49]

If there is one word that you find coming out like a bomb from the Upanishads [a collection of ancient Sanskrit texts containing philosophical concepts central to Hinduism], . . . it is the word fearlessness.[50]

What causes fear? The swami's answer, in line with much classical Hindu teaching, is "ignorance of our own nature." The key insight is that a person's true, immortal Self (*atman*) is identical to the Universal Principle or Universal Self (*Brahman*), the cause of all that is. Each of us is connected to every living being—worms, kangaroos, persons of every description—through the one Self inherent in us all. "Through all mouths, you eat; through all hands, you work; through all eyes, you see."[51]

Fear is intrinsic to the illusion that we are separate from others, a sign that we have not experienced the liberating awareness of being part of a single Reality. "Why should I love my brother?" asks Vivekananda. "Because he and I are one."[52] And how can we fear others once we recognize our essential connection? It is because we don't know our true nature that we draw illusory distinctions—"I am better than you"; "I am different from you"—that lead inexorably to fearful encounters. But once we grasp the unity of all things, how can we fear what we are? In the words of the Upanishads, "Who sees all beings in his own self, and his own self in all beings, loses all fear."[53]

To take this a step further, fear also stems from the illusion that we are separate from God. "But as soon as we have realized that 'I am He, I am the Self of the universe, I am eternally blessed, eternally free'—then will come real love, fear will vanish, and all misery cease."[54] Death is, for most people, the greatest source of fear. But why should we fear dying when there is nothing beyond us that we are not already a part of?

Knowledge of our true self dramatically changes how we live, because "as one thinks, so one becomes."[55] If a person thinks he is bound, then his life will, indeed, be constricted. If a person thinks she is afraid, then her life will, indeed, be marked by suspicion and defensiveness. But, says Vivekananda, it need not be so! His speeches and writings are punctuated with passionate admonitions: "Be fearless." "Be a hero!" "Always say, 'I have no fear.'" "Be not afraid of anything. For the moment you fear you are nobody";[56] that is, you have denied the Self you truly are.

Another indication that one has not attained self-knowledge is attachment to the things of this world, as if possessions or power or academic learning could satisfy the vain, and unnecessary, craving for security. In a letter to a Western follower, the swami quotes a famous medieval Sanskrit poem: "In wealth is the fear of poverty, in knowledge the fear of ignorance, in beauty the fear of age, in fame the fear of backbiters, in success the fear of jealousy, even in body is the fear of death.

Everything in this earth is fraught with fear. He alone is fearless who has given up everything."[57]

Gandhi captures several of these themes in one of his well-known quotations: "One who is free from fear, illusions, and ignorance, free from cravings, possessiveness, and egoism—that one finds peace in self-awareness of the infinite spirit."[58]

How can a person become fearless? To put it another way, how can a person become aware that this apparent world of danger and craving to be secure is an illusion? The path advocated by the Vedanta tradition, and by Ramakrishna and Vivekananda, is meditation—focused concentration on the eternal *atman*, on one's true Self, which is also the all-pervading Principle of the universe.

It would be a mistake, however, to see this as a withdrawal from the world. Vivekananda frequently drew attention to the poverty of his country and to the inhumane treatment of the lower castes; the Ramakrishna Mission promoted health care and engaged in disaster relief; and his writings were a powerful stimulus to India's national awakening. But he eschewed politics, arguing that courageous individuals, people who had become fearless through meditation and consequent self-knowledge, are the essential bedrock of national identity and renewal. We hear this idea reflected in Gandhi's famous instruction: "Let the first act of every morning be to make the following resolve for the day: I shall not fear anyone on earth. I shall fear only God."[59] Only those who are free from fear themselves can effectively lead a reviving nation.

4

The Israeli-Palestinian Conflict

A Case Study

Before offering conclusions and recommendations for how people of religious faith might respond to this fear-dominated society, I want to expand our exploration of fear by presenting a "case study" from a nation other than the United States—a nation living with what feels like intractable conflict. For people in such settings, writes political psychologist Eran Halperin, "fear is much more than a powerful emotion. For most of them it is the dominant state of mind, governing the way they feel, think, act, and make important decisions in their lives."[1] Americans, despite what we hear from some politicians, do not face the daily, immediate threat of violence experienced by some of our global neighbors; but I believe there is still much we can learn from looking closely at one such situation.

The country I have chosen is Israel, for three reasons. First, and most important, there is extensive sociological research regarding the emotional response of Israelis to protracted conflict, research that adds depth and nuance to the discussion of fear in chapter 1. Second, the Israeli-Palestinian conflict, while having to do with competing claims to a piece of land, also involves three of the religions discussed in chapters 2 and 3. Discussion of the role these religions might play in helping to reduce fear and make peace is notable by its absence. Third, I have personal involvement with this situation. Given the politically charged nature of this conflict, it may be good to name this involvement at the outset. I was a foreign exchange student at the Tel Aviv University for the 1969–70 academic year, and returned with my wife to live in Tel Aviv in 1972. My doctoral dissertation dealt with Holocaust literature, and I have taught and practiced Jewish-Christian dialogue throughout my teaching career. At the same time, I have traveled extensively in the West Bank and, through my participation in the National Council of Churches, have met on a number of occasions with Palestinian political and religious leaders. I care deeply about justice for the Palestinian people, including the right to a state of their own on land now occupied by Israel, even as I strongly support Israel's right to exist in peace and security. And, although it is becoming harder, I have believed it possible to affirm both of these things.

This is not to suggest that I am an expert in the Middle East! And I certainly cannot claim to have lived the conflict, with all its tension and anxiety. I was, however, staying in the Old City of Jerusalem when part of the Al-Aqsa mosque was burned in 1969—a time of great fear and anger. I was in Jerusalem in the aftermath of an awful suicide bombing in 2002. And I have witnessed disturbing, fear-tinged encounters between Israeli military police and Palestinians at checkpoints around Bethlehem, Ramallah, and Qalqilyah.

While this chapter will focus primarily on Israeli society, it goes without saying that Palestinian society is also marked by fear. This does not mean, however, that the emotional responses of the populations are symmetrical. At least one scholar has argued that the Israeli "narrative" emphasizes security, which means that isolated events are quickly connected to the larger threat of terrorism, while the Palestinian narrative emphasizes justice, which means that isolated events are quickly connected to the larger picture of Israeli occupation.[2] A more provocative thesis is that set forth by the French scholar Dominique Moïsi. While noting the high level of fear in Israel, Moïsi contends that "humiliation," the sense of being no longer in control, is the driving emotional force in Arab culture, including Palestinian: "Humiliation peaks when you are convinced that the Other has intruded into the private realm of your own life and made you utterly dependent. Humiliation encapsulates a sense of dispossession toward the present and even more so toward the future . . . , a future in which your political, economic, social, cultural conditions are dictated by the Other."[3] Israel, acting out of its own insecurity, feeds right into such humiliation, say Moïsi, with its multiplying roadblocks, checkpoints, and regulations.

Whatever you think of these theories, they are a reminder that "emotions play an important role, not only in individual behavior, but also in societal functioning."[4] And that fear, while universally experienced, is not universally experienced to the same extent or in the same manner.

Fear in Israeli Society

There are, of course, good reasons why Jewish Israelis might feel corporate anxiety in the early years of the twenty-first century. The Hamas Covenant, produced by the Palestinian faction in control of the Gaza Strip, rejects the idea of negotiated peace settlement and calls for the obliteration or dissolution of the state of Israel. The entire region is in political—and, in many places, military—turmoil, and one ardent enemy has at least the long-term capability of producing nuclear weapons. The Second Intifada brought terror to Israeli cities as recently as 2005, and rocket attacks, however inaccurate, are a periodic threat. A high level of public apprehension, say some commentators, is not only understandable but warranted.

Others, however, contend that the objective threat is

overblown. The Egyptian and Jordanian governments seem intent on preserving peaceful borders (even more so since President Abdel Fattah el-Sisi took power in Cairo); the Iranian threat has been reduced, thanks to the diplomatic agreement of 2015; US support remains strong and stable; the Syrian government is preoccupied with civil war and has been stripped of its chemical weapons; and the number of Israeli civilians killed by Palestinians since the end of the intifada in 2005 (203 as of July 2016) is a minuscule fraction of the population.[5]

I will not take sides in this debate over whether Israeli fears are disproportionate to the actual danger (although I will note that the decision, made by some Israeli leaders, to emphasize the level of threat is just that: a decision). My point now is simply that, according to numerous studies, Israeli society is saturated with fear and that living with fear for a prolonged period has significant consequences for the life of any nation.

A good book with which to start our examination is Juliana Ochs's *Security and Suspicion: An Ethnography of Everyday Life in Israel*. Drawing on fieldwork carried out from 2003 to 2005, including the stories of particular Israeli families, Ochs concludes that Israel exists in "a permanent state of emergency,"[6] with security concerns dominating not only political rhetoric but daily activities: whether to go out for pizza, when to ride what bus, how much freedom to allow one's children, whether it is worth the risk to visit relatives in Jerusalem. As Ochs puts it, "fear was a political discourse, but it was also intensely intimate and bodily"—a point expressed in various interviews. "[I]t is as if you have your skin," one woman told her, "and then your clothes, and then there is another something. It's another layer we are wearing. The fear is just there. It is like there is another layer of skin."[7]

All of this, Ochs argues, creates a cycle that is difficult to escape: the obsession with security produces a pervasive sense of vulnerability that leads to an even greater focus on security. In this way, the emphasis on being safe proliferates the very fears it is intended to relieve. Ochs quotes approvingly the social philosopher Zygmunt Bauman: In many modern societies, "fear becomes self-propelling and self-intensifying; it acquires its own momentum and developmental logic and needs little attention and hardly any additional input to spread and grow—unstoppably."[8] Seen through a security filter, other people look suspicious and manageable threats appear perilous. Ochs sees other negative social implications in this obsession with security. For example, a desire for safety has led many—by no means all, but many—Israelis to overlook the troubling effects that their government's policies have on ordinary Palestinians. The decision to build a Separation Barrier or to impose travel restrictions is a political act (other defensible decisions could have been made) with real consequences for Palestinians, who are also afraid. Ochs puts the matter sharply: "Fear was one of the masks Israelis wore to cope with the unease of their implication in the policing of Palestinians, to deal with unspoken guilt about Israel as an occupying power while still seeing themselves as members of a democratic society"[9]—just as many Americans after 9/11 used fear to legitimize their government's use of torture and the high death toll inflicted by their military on Afghan and Iraqi civilians. Fences and checkpoints may have placated some fear, says Ochs, by contributing to the reduction of terrorist attacks; but they also validated the public's anxiety ("look what our nation has to do to protect us"), "transforming emotions of suspicion into traits of good citizenship."[10] Security came to be all-encompassing; all practices related to the occupation and all military-sanctioned violence came under the umbrella of keeping the public secure.

Ochs's work is bolstered by the social analysis of such thinkers as Bauman and David Altheide. "Social life changes," writes Altheide, "when people live behind walls, hire guards, drive armored vehicles . . . , carry mace and handguns, and take martial arts classes. The problem is that these activities reaffirm and help produce a sense of disorder that our actions perpetuate."[11] In other words, a preoccupation with security leads to actions that reinforce our sense of insecurity. Bauman, following the French sociologist Hugues Lagrange, speaks of "derivative fear"—a constant sense of vulnerability.[12] A person who has interiorized such a vision of the world will respond to events as if they are imminently threatening (e.g., with defensiveness or aggression), even when they are not.

Ochs undertook her study during the Second Intifada, obviously a time of heightened public apprehension. Her perceptions are corroborated, however, by subsequent sociological research. In a chapter written for a 2010 publication, two Israeli scholars who are leaders in the field of conflict resolution, Daniel Bar-Tal and Eran Halperin, point out that surveys from the early 1960s already found high levels of fear in the Israeli population. This was intensified with the outbreak of violence following the collapse of peace talks in 2000. In 1999, 58 percent of Israeli Jews reported being afraid or very afraid that they or members of their family would be victims of terror; in 2002, nearly all Israelis (92 percent) felt that way. But surveys indicate that the level of fear remained almost as high even toward the end of the decade, when terrorist attacks had long since stopped in Israel proper. Such studies show, they write, that "fear is a stable and central psychological characteristic of the entire Jewish society in Israel."[13]

I will add, somewhat parenthetically, that not all observers agree with this conclusion. In a 2015 column for the *Huffington Post*, Jewish film director Boaz Yakin contended that "Israel is not afraid. Israel is comfortable"[14]—which explains why it remains politically intransigent. There is no need to negotiate, because the conflict impinges little on the life of the average Israeli. I have heard similar arguments from Jewish friends in the United States, but, as we have seen, they are undercut by studies carried out in Israel itself.

One interesting distinction made in the sociological literature is between physical threats, those that pose potential harm to tangible things (e.g., money, property, human life), and symbolic threats, those that pose potential harm to a community's values or identity. In Israel, this takes the form of an often-referenced "demographic threat"—the perceived danger, felt by many Israeli Jews, of losing the country's Jewish majority and, with that, its distinctive Jewish character. The relatively high Palestinian birthrate does not pose an actual physical threat, at least in any immediate sense, to Jewish life and territory; the threat is "symbolic." The fear felt as a result of such symbolic threat, since the danger is more distant and abstract, is often harder to define and defend. So, Halperin observes, those who experience symbolic threats often try to suggest that they are, in fact, physical[15]—as when Americans who are afraid that immigrants will change the (white, European) character of the nation contend that immigrants are dangerous criminals.

Fear may be particularly powerful and prevalent in the Israeli context because it is so much a part of the national memory (as it is for African Americans and Native Americans in the United States). Traumatic events of Jewish history—from the exodus and the exile in Babylon to Masada, European pogroms, and the Holocaust—help form a national narrative that can make Israelis "oversensitive" to perceived threats. "The lingering memory of the Holocaust," said former foreign minister and historian Amos Elon, "makes Arab [and Iranian] threats of annihilation sound plausible."[16]

It is possible to imagine Israeli leaders attempting to mitigate this siege mentality, attempting to lessen this propensity to read present events in light of the memory of past persecution, in the way that President Roosevelt tried to reduce public fear during the Great Depression. In fact, however, they have tended to propagate it. This example is from the speech of Prime Minister Binyamin Netanyahu on Holocaust Memorial Day, 2009: "We will not allow the Holocaust deniers to carry out another Holocaust against the Jewish people. This is the supreme duty of the state of Israel. This is my supreme duty as Prime Minister of Israel. . . . The world sounds a weak voice against those who advocate erasing Israel."[17]

Former Defense Minister Moshe Ya'alon has condemned

this penchant for exploiting the fears of those who have felt ignored by the governing elite. Israel, Ya'alon has argued, faces no immediate, existential threat, certainly not one it is unprepared to meet. "Thus, it is fitting that the leadership of this country stop scaring the citizenry and stop giving them the feeling that we are standing before a second Holocaust."[18] This criticism has been echoed by another former defense minister, Ehud Barak, who has spoken of Netanyahu's "Hitler-ization of every threat,"[19] and by two former military chiefs of staff, who have inaugurated a new cultural movement aimed at promoting "hope and not fear, when fear is sown in all directions."[20] Instead of seeking to placate public fear, say these critics, current Israeli leaders, unlike many in that nation's pioneering generation, often sympathize with it and present themselves as protectors. This diverts attention from real threats to Israel's existence as a Jewish, democratic state. It is a pattern familiar to contemporary Americans.

Lessons from the Conflict

In addition to what has already been said, I want to draw two other lessons from this case study for our understanding of fear in public life.

The Effect of Fear on Peacemaking

A number of studies have been undertaken in the context of the Israeli-Palestinian conflict to determine how fear affects peacemaking (an obvious value for all major religions). Fear, as we have noted, is a natural response to danger. Indeed, in situations of potential violence, it has a significant functional role, focusing attention on the threat and promoting group solidarity in the face of it.

It is also important to stress that, in the right circumstances, collective fear can advance conflict resolution. Studies done by Halperin and Bar-Tal found that exposure to fear-inducing information about losses inherent in continuation of the conflict between Israel and Palestine generated greater willingness to learn more about possible solutions, to reevaluate current positions, and to endorse compromises than did exposure to hope-inducing information about possible gains derived from a peace agreement. To be more specific, information about the "demographic" threat discussed above led to greater support for a two-state solution—a clear case of fear leading to the embrace of compromise.[21]

Despite this caveat, however, "most conflict resolution scholars see fear as an extremely powerful *barrier* to peace,"[22] for at least three reasons.

First, fear tends to freeze beliefs—about the cause of the conflict, about the intentions of the adversary—making it difficult to entertain new, possibly more factual, information. Opinion polls show, for example, that a majority of Israeli Jews believe Israel has no responsibility for the suffering caused to Palestinians by the war in 1948, despite extensive historical research and personal testimony to the contrary.[23] Often the other group is perceived as more homogenous and extreme than they may, in fact, be. Jewish friends, Israeli and American, who otherwise trust my judgment have dismissed as dangerously naive my personal testimony to the peaceful intentions and diversity of perspectives held by Palestinian acquaintances. According to Bar-Tal, Halperin, and colleagues, peacemaking demands mental flexibility that usually results from the introduction of ideas that are inconsistent with previously held beliefs, ideas that produce internal tension. Fear is usually accompanied by a "cognitive stagnation" that thwarts such flexibility.[24]

Fear does not diminish the desire for information; rather, it affects the kind of information people choose to absorb. Studies focused on the role of fear in shaping attitudes regarding immigration demonstrate that "anxious individuals exhibit biased information processing; they read, remember, and agree with threatening information on issues related to immigrants and immigration."[25] We gravitate to reports that support our bias; needless to say, this is detrimental to conflict resolution.

Second, and closely related, fear makes people (overly) cautious and thus less willing to take the political risks inherent in peace initiatives (e.g., territorial compromises).[26] Fearful leaders, leaders who reflect a fearful public, often fail to respond when the context changes and new opportunities for peace appear. Because the fear has been internalized, situations that cry out for creative, courageous solutions are met with defensive, unilateral ones, even in the absence of immediate threat. An increase in public fear is also associated with a decrease in the number who think resolution of the conflict is even possible. In 1997, 67 percent of Israeli Jews thought peace treaties could bring an end to hostilities. By 2007, this had dropped by more than 40 percentage points.[27] Widespread fear generally means that expectations for the future are based solely on remembered danger. This too is detrimental to peacemaking.

Third, to use Halperin's words, "threat perceptions are consistently among the most important predictors of intergroup prejudice and hostility, exclusionism, political intolerance, political xenophobia, militarism, and support for national security policy."[28] These claims are backed up by an abundance of peer-reviewed studies conducted in Israel and the United States. Studies also confirm the commonsense conclusion that fear increases support for violence, especially when fear is mixed with hatred, contempt, and humiliation.[29] Fearful people and groups react by adopting hostile attitudes toward "outsiders"; this, of course, is detrimental to the resolution of any conflict.

It is interesting to note that the role of religion is seldom mentioned in the various sociological studies. In the collectively written book *Barriers to Peace in the Israeli-Palestinian Conflict*, there is one chapter that underscores how fundamentalist religion is a barrier to compromise.[30] Halperin points to a study, conducted by American and Iranian scholars, that found that when fundamentalist Christians and Muslims were exposed to compassionate teachings from the Bible and the Qur'an, *and* were reminded of their mortality, they expressed less support for violent confrontation between Iran and the United States.[31] It is clear, however, that the teachings of religion regarding fear have not been the subject of much, if any, scholarly research or been employed on behalf of peace.

The Effect of Separation on Fear

The second possible lesson for our understanding of fear has to do with Israel's so-called Separation Barrier, a more-than-four-hundred-mile-long construction project—in many places a twenty-six-foot-high concrete wall—that separates Israeli cities and Jewish settlements from Palestinian communities on the West Bank. Such a barrier was originally proposed by the left-wing Labor Party as a way of demarcating a future Palestinian state. By the time Prime Minister Ehud Barak revived the proposal in 2000, however, the rationale was changing. "It is my assessment," he said at the time, "that we need to separate from the Palestinians. Simply separate ourselves physically—us here and them there."[32] And when Ariel Sharon's right-wing Likud government began construction of the barrier two years later, it was clearly a response to widespread fear in the Israeli public.

One major consequence of this decision was spelled out in a 2014 op-ed article by Ethan Bronner, former Jerusalem bureau chief for the *New York Times*. Bronner observes that only fifteen years ago thousands of Palestinians—40 percent of the Palestinian labor force, by some estimates—worked in Israel. Many Palestinians learned Hebrew, watched Israeli television, even had Israeli friends. Israelis, in turn, ventured on weekends into the West Bank (Moshe Dayan is said to have gone to Nablus at least once a week), where they got their cars fixed, shopped for vegetables, and ate the world's best hummus. They attended weddings of Palestinian employees. Some went into business together.

However, once the Camp David talks failed in 2000 and the Second Intifada erupted, all that went out the window. There quickly developed a common political wisdom, fostered by fear, that the two societies needed to be kept apart, not more fully integrated. In Bronner's experience, communities that once interacted, at least on occasion, now became virtual strangers.[33] This, of course, has led to increased fear of the unknown "other"—just as the historic walls of racial segregation have contributed to fearfulness in such places as Ferguson, Missouri, and the reduction of foot patrols by police in various cities has helped make police and community strangers to one another. This brings to mind Dr. King's dictum: "People fail to get along because they fear each other; [and] they fear each other because they don't know each other."[34]

Bronner's conclusions accord with my own experience, as well as that of other journalists and local residents. For example, Christa Case Bryant made the same observation in a 2015 report for the *Christian Science Monitor*: "Many young Israelis, such as the fourteen-year-old son of a former lifeguard in Gaza, can't remember talking with a Palestinian face to face. . . . With the two populations cut off from each other, Israelis often don't have a personal frame of reference against which to compare the rhetoric used in times of conflict."[35] "[W]e live so close to each other," said one participant in a Palestinian-Israeli roundtable discussion published in *Harper's*, "yet we know so little about each other. You used to know us as laborers, doing the labor Israelis didn't want to do, and now you know us as homicide bombers. And we only know you as colonists and occupiers."[36]

There is considerable evidence that, while separation may reduce short-term fear, it only exacerbates the long-term conflict and ultimately intensifies anxiety. "You don't see Palestinians, so you can envision them however you want," says Bar-Tal. "What people are afraid of the most is the unknown."[37] In a chapter summarizing recent sociological studies, published in 2010, Bar-Tal, Halperin, and Oren conclude that "negative stereotyping of the Palestinians has become more common since 2000,"[38] reaching unprecedented levels. A study of Israeli Jews in 2008 found that 77 percent of the respondents believe that

Arabs, including Palestinians, have little regard for human life, and 79 percent believe they are always dishonest.[39] Let's make the point positively. Work done by Bar-Tal and colleagues in the field of conflict resolution confirms that "differentiation" is a key to peacemaking.[40] Differentiation involves a recognition that the foe is not a uniformly hostile monolith but includes subgroups that may hold values similar to one's own and that also favor peace. Israeli society, to take that example, includes numerous groups, including B'Tselem and Rabbis for Human Rights, who work constantly to promote justice for Palestinians. Beyond that, the "other" is made up of individuals with ordinary human needs, concerns, aspirations. This differentiating focus on the diversity of the other, on individuals within the other, helps reduce fear by perceiving areas of commonality. Such differentiation is possible, of course, only if the conflicting parties have contact with one another. "The most useful commodity for the merchants of war and hatred," writes Roger Cohen with regard to this conflict, "is fear." What we need, he argues, are "interceptors of fear," who help their group imagine how the world looks through the eyes of those on the other side of the wall.[41]

This contention is corroborated by a study of "Seeds of Peace," which for a quarter century has brought Palestinian and Israeli teenagers to a summer camp in Maine—three weeks of shared activities and intensive, guided conversation. In 2016, the 159 campers also included youth from Egypt, Jordan, and the United States. Social scientists Juliana Schroeder and Jane Risen studied the program for four years, testing whether personal contact with those on "the other side of the wall" produced a measurable and sustained change in attitude. Their results, published in 2014, are encouraging: "From pre-camp to post-camp, we found that Israeli and Palestinian teenagers alike reported feeling more positive toward, close with, similar to, and trusting of the other side. On average, for all of these questions, the teenagers moved up almost a full point on the scale from where they started, a statistically significant change.

They also reported feeling more optimistic about the likelihood of peace and more committed to working for peace."[42] The researchers found that these changes persisted a year after the summer experience, especially for those who formed at least one close relationship.

In 2001, some 120 former participants in this program—coming from the Middle East, South Asia, the Balkans, Cyprus, and the United States—issued their own "charter." We grew up, they wrote, in "tense, fearful environments" and arrived at the camp "full of stereotypes and prejudices against our enemy." After the three weeks together, however, "we returned home with an understanding of the other side and acceptance of our common humanity. We learned that we are strong together."[43]

As I write this chapter, building a wall along the United States's southern border has become a prominent issue in the 2016 presidential campaign. And the United States is not alone. "In symbolic terms," writes Dominique Moïsi, "the fall of the Berlin Wall in 1989 was the culmination of a European culture of hope, with people across the continent celebrating the fall of a wall that had divided them." But now, a quarter century later, "Europeans [give] the impression of wishing to see the erection of walls that would separate them from the external world—with its millions of competitors, its thousands of immigrants, its hundreds of terrorists."[44] It is a vivid indication, as he sees it, that the West has become a "culture of fear."

Will separating barriers in the long run make us safer? The Israeli experience should at least give our politicians pause. The question I am asking, however, is slightly different: Don't our religious traditions speak truth when they promote interdependence as an antidote to fear? Don't our religions teach the importance of seeing the other as differentiated persons—persons who not only have their own anxieties but their own inherent worth and dignity? I firmly believe that the churches in the United States and the U.S.S.R. contributed to the fall of the Berlin Wall through person-to-person visits and exchanges.

I have no doubt that churches helped end the era of apartheid by putting a human face, for people in Europe and America, on the suffering of black South Africans. Don't religious communities have a similar witness to make to the reality of human interdependence in *this* fearful era?

A Concluding Unscientific Postscript

Throughout this chapter, we have listened to the results of social-scientific research. I will end it by turning to the astonishingly prescient, and frightening, insights of an Israeli novelist. David Grossman is one of Israel's leading writers, known internationally for such novels as *To the End of the Land*, *The Smile of the Lamb*, and *Falling Out of Time*. He is also a former soldier, the father of a soldier who was killed in 2006 during fighting in southern Lebanon, and an activist who has spoken out forcefully for a just, negotiated settlement with the Palestinians.

Two weeks after the attacks of 9/11, Grossman wrote an article for *The Age* newspaper in Melbourne, Australia, in which he predicted, on the basis of his experience as an Israeli, what other societies will look like if and when fear becomes dominant:

> Gradually, Americans, Europeans, and others will find themselves surrounded by an endless number of security systems. These systems are meant to defend people, but actually make them feel more upset and less secure. Myriad policemen, security guards, special forces troops, and overt and covert detectives will be stationed at the entrances to cinemas, theaters, and shopping centers. Guards will check those who enter schools and preschools. . . .
>
> The frightened civilian quickly composes his own internal mechanism that identifies and catalogues strangers by their racial/national/ethnic traits. Like it or not, he becomes more racist. It is not hard to predict that, under such conditions, the political parties that feed off racism will flourish.[45]

The Israeli experience indicates that public life will be diminished, since so much energy and creativity that could have gone into improving the quality of life are channeled into security. Even more tragically, as he sees it, "the individual soul also will become enveloped by this coarse, stiff veneer. That is the immediate result of living in fear, in suspicion of every unfamiliar person. . . . It is painful to admit," Grossman concludes, "but in a certain sense terror always succeeds. The war against it, and the process of becoming accustomed to what it does with our lives, slowly perverts all that is precious and human."

5

Recommendations
for Religious Communities

Daring the course of writing this book, I had dinner with a group of friends, most of whom grew up in some church but are not now active in any religious community. In response to their questions, I described my thesis: that religions have a common witness to make against the often-misguided fear that is so prevalent in contemporary America. The ensuing conversation included comments like these:

> Well, you'll have to convince me! The way I see it, religion is a big part of the problem. Every time you turn around there's a story of a Christian shooting up a Planned Parenthood clinic in the name of God, or Muslims trying to terrorize people based on some twisted understanding of their faith. Even the Buddhists are doing it in Myanmar! It seems to me that religion causes at least as much fear as it relieves.

> People fight for lots of reasons, but it's always more frightening when religion gets involved. Then it's turned into a fight between good and evil—no compromise possible.

I know there are compassionate believers, but the people who talk about their religion in public are often pretty scary! They seem so intolerant of those who don't believe the way they do—even demonize them. And that sure as hell frightens me!

I suppose religion gives some people a sense of protection, although I don't see how that gets at the problem of fear in society.

What I remember from Sunday school is a picture of Satan—horns, hooves, pitchfork—that I found terrifying! Church can make you afraid. Just ask our friends who are gay.

It is a great understatement to say that I find such statements painful. Of course, they are so painful because there is much in them that is true. Religion, not unreasonably, is associated in many people's minds with fear.

You can think of this book, then, as a call to renewal. As I have tried to show, the great world religions *at their best* have a message that challenges the fear contagion of our era. Their teachings, as we have seen, are certainly not identical; but all of them see fear as often hazardous to the health of human society, and offer ways of overcoming it. The question I am asking is whether Bahá'ís, Buddhists, Christians, Hindus, Jews, Muslims, Sikhs, and other people of religious faith can recover this fear-diminishing heart of their proclamation—and then speak out together.

Another problem, however, is that those communities (I am thinking especially of churches) most likely to respond positively to what I have just said often live fearfully themselves: afraid of losing members, afraid of declining revenue, afraid of losing a familiar sense of identity, afraid of losing even more status and influence in the culture. So they—we—act defensively, emphasizing our particular message, not what we have in common with others, fearfully protecting what we have rather than risking it in a bold, countercultural witness against fear.

All of this is a reminder that, while some fear is certainly justified and may even be necessary in times of crisis, much fear is unwarranted and rooted in self-centeredness. If our well-being is gained at the expense of others, then it is nearly inevitable that we will live anxiously. If our status depends on the depreciation of others, then we will live anxiously. If our lifestyle is built on a use of resources that threatens the planet, then we will live anxiously. If our security is based on treating others as enemies, then we will live anxiously. If our sense of community is dependent on the exclusion of others, then we will live anxiously. And if our focus is on the preeminence of our religious group, on beating the religious competition, rather than on the flourishing of this one divinely given creation, then we will surely live anxiously. And we will not be the witness we can and should be against fear.

In the Christian New Testament, there is a passage that speaks directly to our theme: "There is no fear in love, but perfect love casts out fear." This is followed quickly by: "We love because God first loved us" (1 John 4:18–19). Speaking now as a Christian, I believe that when our love grows from our trust in God, the One who has loved us so perfectly, then it is incompatible with fear; it casts it out. But, conversely, human fear can also cast out love. Unlike grief or empathy, fear is an emotion that does not recognize the full reality of others. It is fundamentally narcissistic, and thus thwarts compassionate identification with those "outside."[1] Shining the spotlight only on what will make me and my group secure casts others into darkness.

Corey Robin, in his book *Fear: The History of a Political Idea*, stresses that fear cannot be the ground of our politics; political vision must be built on freedom and equality.[2] In the same way, fear cannot be the ground of healthy religion— unless by fear we mean awe in the presence of that which is transcendent. Our religious vision must be built on love and hope. Thus the level of anxiety in a religious community may well be an indication of its need for renewal, just as an emphasis on human interdependence, along with a refusal to find security in things other than the Divine, is a sign of vitality and health.

One way religious communities can model a world without fear is by refusing to live in fearful isolation from one another. Religions, in the context of the United States, do cooperate at times with one another (in some places more than others) and, especially at the national level, engage in occasional shared advocacy on behalf of common social and ecological concerns. Much of the political advocacy carried out by the National Council of Churches during my years as general secretary was done with organizations representing other religions.

I am suggesting, however, that our witness could be even more profound if we addressed together the deep currents of our culture—starting with fear. Whatever the legislative debate about immigration, we need to help envision a society that is not afraid to welcome strangers. Whatever the legislative debate about guns, we need to help envision a society in which courage is associated not with violence but with peacemaking. Whatever the legislative debate about national security, we need to help envision a society that is not afraid to think in terms of human interdependence, not just unilateral defense. This witness can be made with full credibility only when we make it alongside those who worship in ways unlike our own.

Let's Get Specific

What might this mean more concretely? Following is a list of ten things religious communities might do to challenge the narrative of fear. The first five are steps each community could take on its own; the second five steps we could take together as interfaith partners. I urge readers, however, to think of this not simply as a checklist of actions to be accomplished but

as visible expressions of religion that helps cast out fear. You
might even see them as signs of our own renewal.
1. *In each of our communities, teach what our own tradition
has said about fear and how to diminish it.*
Of course, it is also important to learn what other religions
have taught; but even before that, it is crucial to understand
our own heritage. The preceding chapters in this book hopefully provide a starting point for such teaching, and this book
contains a study guide to help facilitate congregational discussion and learning. My own experience tells me that people in
our churches, mosques, synagogues, and temples are fed up
with the fear-mongering in our society and eager to say no to it
as people of faith. While reading a book about all this is good
(at least I hope so!), discussion with other members of our
community is an essential next step.
2. *Become more intentional about seeing our congregations
as places where fears can be shared and discussed.*
Our religious communities are not only teaching centers;
they are also places where people find fellowship, comfort, and
support. Scott Bader-Saye expresses this in some detail with
specific reference to Christians:

> The church, the body of Christ, is the place where, through
> baptism, we have already faced death, our greatest fear, and
> seen it overcome. And so we ought to exist as a gathering in
> which fears can be expressed honestly, since we no longer
> believe they can control us. If giving voice to fear is one way
> of keeping fear from controlling us, then the church needs
> to become a place where we are not embarrassed to hear
> the fears of others or to share our own. Indeed, it needs to
> become a place that helps us find the words to bring fear out
> of the "wordless darkness." This may happen through small
> groups and support groups where we come to know and trust
> one another well enough to share our fears. It may happen
> through the liturgy, especially the psalms of lament, which
> allow us to give voice together to our fears and anxieties. It
> may happen in the proclamation, as preachers name from

the pulpit the fears that grip us. And when it does happen, we will begin to become communities of courage precisely because we have found ways to name, and thus confront, the fears that keep us from living fully and joyfully.[3]

I now begin Sunday Bible studies at the congregation where I am a member by asking, "What fear do you bring with you as we gather this morning?" We find that the ensuing conversation often puts our fears in perspective and shifts the focus away from ourselves to the more spiritual question of what makes our neighbors afraid.

3. *Encourage firsthand knowledge of other religions and cultures.*

Experience from the Israeli-Palestinian conflict, discussed in the previous chapter, underscores that people often fear what they don't know. In this era when Muslims have become the focus of much anxiety and misinformation, other religious communities may want to invite a Muslim speaker or organize a tour of a local mosque. Mosques and Islamic centers will likely have extensive information on Islam, as well as people to lead tours and answer questions. In my experience, fear almost inevitably decreases with such exposure.

Encounter with persons of other religions or cultures may also reveal what causes *them* to be afraid. I live in San Diego, where Mexican and Mexican American colleagues report high levels of anxiety throughout their communities with regard to immigration. Even those who are legal residents or US citizens have friends, family members, or other members of their congregation who live in daily fear of deportation. One sign that our church or temple or synagogue or mosque is serious about opposing fear is an active commitment to help relieve the understandable fear felt by others—in this case, at least as I see it, by advocating for comprehensive, humane reform of immigration policies.

4. *In our own communities, practice dialogue with persons with whom we genuinely disagree.*

I suspect that many people reading this book will welcome the idea of meeting people of other religions and cultures but will find it harder to engage constructively with persons of their own tradition whose ideological perspectives they find troubling. To use my own religion as an example, Christians who identify themselves as politically liberal or conservative will probably find it easier to relate to like-minded Jews or Muslims or Buddhists than to Christians who disagree with them on such issues as gun control or same-sex marriage. As a result, most of us likely spend far more time talking *about* these political, ideological opponents than talking *with* them—which can increase not only anger (and blood pressure) but anxiety. It is in our efforts to defeat or disprove ideological opponents that we often resort to fear. "If *that* idea prevails, then we are headed for disaster!"

So communities that seek to counter the prevalence of fear in public life need, in my judgment, to practice dialogue with those with whom they genuinely disagree. Think of this as a spiritual discipline—not necessarily to reach agreement, but to attempt to see the world through their eyes. There are many "guidelines for dialogue" available, all of which emphasize listening respectfully and carefully to others and speaking honestly about your own position and the reasons why you hold it.[4] In addition to these, the following principles or guidelines have been particularly important in my own ecumenical and interfaith ministry:

- Allow others to define themselves and their positions on the issues in their own terms. Assuming in advance that we know what the other will say leads almost inevitably to caricaturing and inaccurate generalizations. Fear is confronted when we follow this version of the Golden Rule: Try to understand others as you hope to be understood by them.
- Be sensitive to the fears and pressures that weigh on the other. For example, when Jews and Christians meet in this country to talk about the conflict in the Middle East, it is

important for the Christians to understand how the fears of Jews in Haifa and Jerusalem weigh on their Jewish compatriots in America, and for the American Jews to understand that the fears of Christians in Bethlehem and Ramallah may well be on the minds of American Christians. In the debate over gun violence, one party may fear armed criminals, while another fears a proliferation of arms in the general public. Don't both deserve to be taken seriously?

- Recognize that different positions are often better understood as points on a continuum than as polar opposites. To speak again of gun violence, there is a lot of room between (a) opposing all gun regulation and (b) severely restricting private ownership of firearms. Fear-mongering usually comes from the extremes, while most of us are somewhere in the middle.
- Focus on the issues without questioning the motives, intelligence, or integrity of those who hold a different position. I regret even needing to say this! But the presidential campaign, under way as I write, shows us how often it is violated.
- Be willing to be changed by the dialogue, which is a way of insisting that genuine dialogue is not for the sake of defending predetermined convictions.

5. *Make welcoming the stranger a key part of the identity of our religious communities.*

This would be a significant challenge to the culture of fear. For much of human history, strangers have been a source of fear, objects of suspicion—which may be why every world religion has teachings that explicitly instruct its followers to welcome strangers.

- From the Upanishads (the texts that are the wellspring of Hindu religion and philosophy): "Let a person never turn away a stranger from his house, that is the rule. Therefore, a man should, by all means, acquire much food, for good people say to the stranger: 'There is enough food for you.'"[5]
- From the Qur'an: "Be kind to parents, and the near kinsman, and to orphans, and to the needy, and to the neighbor

who is of kin, and to the neighbor who is a stranger, and to the companion at your side, and to the traveler."[6]

- From the Tanakh (Hebrew Scripture): "The alien [the Hebrew word is *ger*, which can also be translated "stranger"] who resides with you shall be to you as the citizen among you; you shall love the alien as yourself, for you were aliens in the land of Egypt."[7]

- From the Christian New Testament: "Then the king [Jesus] will say to those at his right hand, 'Come, you that are blessed by my Father, inherit the kingdom prepared for you from the foundation of the world; for I was hungry and you gave me food, I was thirsty and you gave me something to drink, I was a stranger and you welcomed me. . . .'"[8]

It almost goes without saying that fear is toxic to a spirit of hospitality; conversely, welcoming those who are in some fundamental way unlike ourselves can be an antidote to fear. My congregation is part of the Interfaith Shelter Network in San Diego. For two weeks each year, sometimes more, we welcome people who are homeless into our facility and our community, providing beds and showers and food. There is no doubt that this helps lessen our fear of the homeless and increases our identification with their struggles. We are learning that true welcome doesn't insist that strangers become grateful allies. It simply enables them to feel at home; if we are open, this enables us to feel at home with them. A culture of fear tells us not to risk vulnerability or generosity, because resources can be scarce and strangers can be dangerous. The practice of hospitality says that we, as people of faith, will live a different way.[9]

6. *As people of religious faith, seek regular, constructive interfaith relationships.*

This action is itself a visible rejection of the culture of fear. People of different religious backgrounds may well know one another as business colleagues or fellow students or members of a civic organization, but historically we have not known one another as people of faith. Indeed, it is the religious identity of other people—their beliefs, their rituals, their clothing and symbols—that often seems particularly foreign, even frightening. Thus it is of great importance that, in this generation, we join *as religious believers* in witness to the common good. Interfaith relations also hold the possibility of learning from one another, including about how to respond to the problem of fear! As we have seen, a person need not convert to another religion in order to find answers to this problem; all of the major religions have important teachings on this subject. But that doesn't preclude gaining insights from the witness of others in the interfaith community.

Nearly all major US cities now have interfaith organizations that welcome the participation of congregations and individuals. I urge readers to get actively involved, if you aren't already, in such organizations. Obviously, I hope interfaith partnerships will make public opposition to fear an explicit part of their agendas. But even if they don't, their very existence as places where people of different religions can shed their defensiveness is a witness to a culture in which fearful suspicion is the order of the day.

7. *As people of religious faith, speak out together against fear-mongering in public life.*

The biggest divide in US political life may now be between those who insist on using scare tactics to further their agenda or denigrate their opponents and those (their ranks seem to be thinning) who don't. People of faith, without pushing a partisan agenda, can demand a higher standard. For example, in December 2015, national leaders from a wide variety of religious communities joined in denouncing anti-Muslim rhetoric. Their statement included this paragraph:

> Good citizens must speak out. As faith and community leaders who value our own freedom of religion, we state unequivocally that we love our Muslim siblings in humanity. They serve our communities as doctors, lawyers, teachers, engineers, journalists, first responders, and as members of the U.S. Armed Forces and Congress. Muslims are our

equals. They are no different from anyone else pursuing the American dream. Together, we are proud Americans. Together, we choose freedom not fear.[10]

Disseminate such statements locally. Object when local politicians use fear to garner support. Object that local media sensationalize crime. If possible, do so together.

8. *As people of religious faith, join in prayer with one another, when possible.*

This, some would say, should be first on the list, if only to remind us that we are not the center of the universe, the measure of all things. Fear, as we have noted, is self-centered; prayer can never be, because it is directed beyond ourselves to that which alone is Holy, Ultimate, Real. Prayer in each of our traditions is understood as a way of letting go of fear. How much more so, when it is done together.

Having said this, I need to add that interfaith prayer is potentially difficult because it easily assumes the form of whatever group is locally dominant. It is particularly tough when the interreligious community includes Buddhists, a tradition often described as nontheistic because it doesn't affirm a Creator Deity to whom humans pray. I believe, however, that with appropriate sensitivity interfaith prayer can be a powerful check on unwarranted anxiety. It reinforces the sense of human interdependence as we pray for and with other parts of the human family. It is a sign that we trust ultimately in God (by whatever name) and not in the things we accumulate to ensure our security.

Prayer is not a substitute for practical acts of solidarity and shared service; rather, it mobilizes our imagination to envision the world as God would have it. Prayer is not a way of stifling protest; it is itself a profound protest against the reduction of life to self-interest and self-defense.

9. *As people of religious faith, emphasize together the importance of human interdependence.*

The term "globalization" generally refers to the easy flow

of capital, goods, services, and information across national borders that is so characteristic of this era. While this process contributes to human integration, it also often results in the diminishment of local cultures and economies, leaving people with the feeling that their well-being is determined by forces far removed from their knowledge or control—as when U.S. manufacturing jobs are moved to other countries. It is easy to see why globalization has been a source of fear for many persons.

By contrast, interdependence, at least as used by religious groups, refers to the conviction that human beings, in all our diversity, belong to one another in this divinely given creation. It connotes solidarity in suffering and celebration, a desire to understand one another more fully, a willingness to seek areas of commonality—all of which is a counterwitness to fear. Every act of interfaith engagement is a visible indication of human interdependence; but I am suggesting that this should also be a constant and explicit theme when we meet as people of faith.

There is, however, a particularly difficult side to the practice of interdependence, and that is a willingness to see "enemies" too as human beings. The philosopher Firmin DeBrabander puts it this way:

> [I]f we should look at our opponents in this War on Terror and recognize them for what they are—people with personal tragedies and fears, motivated by anger, nourished on prejudiced and incomplete accounts of America . . .—this would erode our paralyzing fear and the violent tendencies it inspires and excuses. We must see them as more than mere black holes of unwavering malice. An abstracted enemy balloons into an indomitable specter and elicits unmanageable levels of fear, with irrationalities that ripple through society.[11]

Interdependence does not mean a failure to condemn evil or an unwillingness to resist it; but it does mean a resistance to us-them thinking that only contributes to fear.

*10. As people of religious faith, lift up together the impor-
tance of, and the real basis for, hope.*
The opposite of fear is not invulnerability; people in guarded
enclaves are often afraid. The opposite of fear is hope, an ori-
entation to the future marked not by anticipated danger but
anticipated fulfillment. It takes intentional effort, however,
to live hopefully rather than fearfully. Hope is a conscious,
cognitive activity, involving such cognitive skills as creativity,
flexibility, and imagination. Fear is a more automatic, unconscious emotion. The significance of this contrast is stated
succinctly by the Israeli scholar Daniel Bar-Tal: "Because
hope is based on thinking, it can be seriously impeded by
the spontaneous and unconscious interference of fear."[12] In
other words, it is not easy to live hopefully when the cultural
narrative is one of fear; this is why we need the reinforcement
of other believers.

Hope, of course, is not the same as optimism. Still, it is telling that, as fear has increased, optimism (expectation of a better future based on an assessment of the present) has become
"uncool." The editorial in the *New York Times* that used this
descriptor cites a host of social indicators in support of their
claim that "the country is, on the whole, in the best shape it's
ever been in."[13] Yet polls show that the national mood is one
of deep pessimism about America's future. Problems, some
of which are admittedly large, are not seen in the current climate as challenges to be overcome but as proof of the country's
social decay. Such pessimism invites further fear-mongering.
If things really are so bad, then we do need walls to keep out
immigrants and guns to protect us from criminals and a scaling
back of civil rights in the name of security.

I want to be clear. The religious traditions named in this
book are not blind to the realities of the world. There are real
reasons for some people in some places to be fearful, a fact
that should be troubling to all of us. Not a single author I have
quoted denies the threat posed by terrorism or nuclear weapons or discrimination or unemployment or crime or ecological

destruction. But these religions, at their best, refuse to define life as a zero-sum game in which our security is gained at the expense of others. Fear is part of human life. But, at their best, our varied traditions have said we will not be ruled by fear or allow our view of the world to be defined by it. Because we know that life is interrelated, we will not allow fear to divide the human family. Because we are not our own creators, there is good reason to be hopeful.

What Will the Future Look Like?

In premodern Europe, fear was ubiquitous: fear of disease and natural disaster, fear of capricious rulers, fear of witches and other creatures that haunted the imagination, fear of religious damnation. The vision expressed by champions of Western modernity was of "a time free of all that stuff of which fears are made."[14] Indeed, astonishing progress has been made in this direction. Illnesses that once cut short so many lives are now banished thanks to vaccines or treated through other advances in medicine. The natural world, while not "controlled," is far, far better understood (the unknown has always been fertile ground for anxiety), and we are now able to predict storms and build houses to withstand them. Programs such as Social Security protect against penury in old age, a pervasive fear for so many of our ancestors. Democracy, however frustrating it can sometimes be, has given ordinary people a say in decisions that affect their lives.[15]

So it is ironic that fear is now ubiquitous in postmodern Western culture. Enlightenment thinkers saw things that make us afraid as problems to be overcome. Here in the twenty-first century, fear is again more all-pervasive, as if we are always at risk. Bauman pointedly names the irony of our situation: We who live in the most "developed" parts of the world "are 'objectively' the most secure people in the history of humanity."[16] We are protected, as no other society ever has been, against the forces of nature, the inherent weaknesses of our bodies, and the aggression of other people. Yet it is in our Western, developed countries

> that the addiction to fear and the securitarian obsession have made the most spectacular careers in recent years. Contrary to the objective evidence, it is the people who live in the greatest comfort on record, more cosseted and pampered than any other people in history, who feel more threatened, insecure and frightened, more inclined to panic, and more passionate about everything related to security and safety than people in most other societies past and present.[17]

Those who make security the goal will never have enough.

The costs for a society suffering from excessive fear are tremendous. Peter Stearns names them this way in his book *American Fear*:

• *"Fear can worsen the quality of life."*[18] Traditional societies, writes Stearns, "overdosed on fatalism," failing to take steps that could have prevented mishaps. Our society, however, has moved too far in the other direction, becoming overly anxious about remote risks. Such anxiety, egged on by the social context, means that many people lead restricted lives—afraid to travel, constantly afraid of disease, afraid to go out after dark.

• *"Excessive fear distorts."*[19] Fear, he notes, creates a willingness to believe inaccurate information—immigrants are a drain on social welfare, violent crime is on the rise, Sharia law is a threat to the Constitution, Iraq has weapons of mass destruction—often with disastrous consequences for public policy. It also leads to misplaced reactions, for example, the spike in sales of home security systems in the days after 9/11—as if a burglar alarm would deter Bin Laden.

• *"Excessive fear can lead not only to misguided decisions, but to measures that are actually counterproductive."*[20] Studies show that exaggerated fears of breast cancer can cause women to resist medical checkups, which increases the risk to their health. Exaggerated fear of the danger posed by immigrants and refugees has led to the antagonism or exclusion of many persons who could have greatly contributed to this nation. Exaggerated fears of crime resulted in mandatory sentencing requirements that have packed our prisons, draining resources needed for such things as education. Exaggerated fear of terrorism led this country's leaders to condone torture, which greatly damaged our moral authority with other nations. In the aftermath of 9/11, air travel dropped dramatically, even though automobile travel, the usual alternative, is many times more dangerous. One scholar calculates that 1,595 people were killed in car crashes as a direct result of the public's post-9/11 fear of flying.[21]

• *"Fear can distort focus, drawing disproportionate attention to the apparent fear source at the expense of other issues of equal or possibly greater importance."*[22] Excessive fear, in Stearns's analysis, means that we often try to prevent the past from recurring rather than undertaking a balanced assessment of future threats. The United States, for example, has spent massive resources on airport security since 2001 but given relatively little attention to the security of trains, subways, ships, and roadways.

Thirty years ago, one of my professors at the University of Chicago, Langdon Gilkey, wrote this prescient paragraph:

> [I]f the level of anxiety within our common life rises, surprising things can happen, as they happened to other cultures repeatedly in this [twentieth] century: Japanese, German, Italian, Russian, Chinese, Islamic—to name a few. Despite our confidence in ourselves [more evident in 1981 than today!], we are by no means immune to this disease; and when the fever of anxiety gets high enough, even constitutional safeguards, not to mention diversity of custom and of ecclesiastical centers, may not be sufficient.[23]

This leads me to ask: What will American society look like thirty years from now? Some scholars argue that excessive fear has become a permanent dimension of postmodern culture, and thus envision a country in 2050 marked by suspicion of outsiders, an increasingly armed and militarized society that has walls to protect our borders and gates to protect our communities, a country skeptical about the future. But is this really inevitable? Isn't it possible to imagine a United States in 2050 in which most people have greater appreciation for diversity, in which there is greater hopefulness about addressing complex challenges? Isn't it possible to resist the narrative of fear?

The question posed by this book is whether religion—long a source of fear, at least for many in the West—might in our era provide a counterwitness to it. Of course, there will continue to be religious leaders who preach punishment more than grace, fear more than hope. But as I have tried to show, at the core of the world's major religions is a different message: Be not afraid! It is a word for our time.

A Guide for Study

My hope in writing this brief book about such a pressing issue is that, in addition to being read by individuals, *The Witness of Religion in an Age of Fear* will be used as the basis for study in congregations, religious book circles, and interfaith organizations and discussion groups. The following questions and other suggestions for group conversation are provided with that goal in mind.

In the first section below, I offer questions related to the introduction and each of the five chapters. This suggests a discussion in six sessions; but a group could obviously alter this in any number of ways. You might, for example, want to combine your discussion of the introduction and chapter 1 in one session on "the culture of fear," spend more time on chapters 2 and 3 ("the religious understanding of fear"), and end with a single session on chapters 4 and 5 ("our response to the problem"). Some groups, of course, will need to limit their discussion to one or two sessions. Thus, in the second section below, I offer abbreviated lists of questions, one for an interfaith group and another for a group that has only Christian participants.

It probably could go without saying that the studies will be more interesting and informative if your group invites speakers from other religious traditions and/or visits other religious communities, arranging in advance for a discussion with the imam, priest, rabbi, minister, or other religious leader. Fear is a topic of concern to us all! Perhaps it can also be the occasion for bringing people together. Discussion leaders (and others) may wish to do additional reading on this subject. The most accessible and comprehensive examination of fear in American society is Barry Glassner's *The Culture of Fear* (New York: Basic Books, 1999). Be sure to get the Tenth Anniversary Edition, which, as the cover says, is "updated for our post 9/11 world." For Christian groups, Scott Bader-Saye's *Following Jesus in a Culture of Fear* (Grand Rapids: Brazos Press, 2007) is an excellent resource. Finally, some readers of this book may want to focus more on how to overcome fear in their personal lives. A book for them may be Rabbi Harold Kushner's *Conquering Fear* (New York: Anchor Books, 2009).

Questions and Discussion Suggestions for Each of the Chapters

Introduction

1. What is good about fear? Give examples, from your own life or that of the society, of fears that seem particularly warranted. How do you distinguish (to use Dr. King's terms) "normal fear" from "abnormal fear"?
2. Imagine the fears of someone or some group in a situation different from your own. What groups, in your opinion, have most reason to be afraid? Have you seen fear used as a tool by those with power to keep others down?
3. Do you agree that religion and fear have often gone hand in hand? Is it legitimate for a religion to use the fear of hell or the fear of God to promote moral behavior? You may want to read the statements at the beginning of chapter 5 in connection with this question. Do any of those statements ring true?
4. Discuss the distinction between fear and anxiety. How do you respond to this statement (p. 7): "A free-floating anxiety over the changing demographics of U.S. society finds outlet in a fear of immigrants and refugees—Mexicans and Central Americans at one moment, Middle Easterners at another"?

5. Do you agree that "there is one America united by fear and another united by the fear of fear" (p. 8)?

Your group may want to identify a source of anxiety for members of your community (e.g., health care or crime) and invite a guest speaker who can shed light on the issue.

Chapter 1

1. Discuss the basic thesis of this chapter: that "the problem . . . is not that we have fears (some of which may well be warranted), but that we live in a *state* of fear that affects the way we see the world, creating anxiety that is not in proportion to actual danger" (p. 18). What parts of the chapter (what statistics) did you find most surprising or disturbing? Give examples from your experience of political rhetoric, news stories, or advertisements that play on the public's fear.

2. Given the political climate, several statements in this chapter are likely to stir up a lively discussion! For example:
   - "In our time, disastrous things have been done in the name of safety" (p. 10).
   - "Guns do not liberate us from fear. They are a symptom of fear's domination over society" (p. 16).
   - "[T]his is one of the biggest problems between African Americans and the police, that we are both afraid of one another, and so we act irrationally" (p. 17).
   - "We are the healthiest, wealthiest, and most long-lived people in history. And we are increasingly afraid. . . . It seems the less we have to fear, the more we fear" (p. 26).

Such statements, even the ones by other people, reflect my own perspective, which I have tried to support in this chapter. It would be foolish, however, not to acknowledge that there are other defensible perspectives! This is an opportunity for your group to discuss your differences of opinion—and to do so without animosity or fear. The guidelines for dialogue listed in chapter 5 (pp. 87–88) may be useful.

3. Assuming that we do live in a "culture of fear," why is this so? Three theories are presented in this chapter:
   - that approaches to education and child-rearing now emphasize the avoidance of risk, leaving people unprepared to deal appropriately with threat;
   - that US society is in the midst of a period of rapid, disorienting change when the world feels dangerously out of control and unfamiliar to many of our contemporaries;
   - that it is in the interest of various groups, especially the media and politicians, to keep the public on edge.
   Do you find any of these explanations convincing? What others come to mind?

4. If specific fears are largely learned (p. 21), how are they taught? Think of an example in your life when you learned to be afraid of something or someone. How did you learn it?

The discussion leader may want to invite group members to bring articles, advertisements, and so forth that demonstrate the prevalence of fear or seem intended to encourage it.

Chapter 2

1. This chapter argues that Christianity and Judaism (and other religions, as we see in the next chapter) challenge the fearfulness of human society by calling us (1) to trust in God for security, rather than in things of our own making, and (2) to affirm the interdependence of the human family as a counter to the present overemphasis on protection of our family, group, or nation. Discuss the importance, and the difficulty, of living by these teachings.

2. How do you understand the "fear of the Lord"? Does the discussion in this chapter (pp. 29–31) help make sense of this biblical phrase? How does fearing God relieve us of earthly fears?

3. Do you agree with the statement "security pursued through military force, seen through the lens of biblical religion, is the surest path to lasting insecurity—to perpetual fear" (p. 32)? Is it possible to live in the world, with all its violence (often suffered by the most vulnerable members of human society), and still trust in God more than military for our security? Is the "abundance" enjoyed by many in the United States also a form of violence against the world's poor?

4. Paul Tillich, like many writers and philosophers in the middle years of the twentieth century, wrote about the "anxiety of meaninglessness" stemming from a sense that structures and beliefs that have long provided meaning and coherence to life are now disintegrating (pp. 38–39). Does this ring true for you today? Do you think the loss of a spiritual center helps account, at least in part, for the "culture wars" of recent decades?

5. The bishops of The United Methodist Church contend that "following Jesus leads to radical insecurity" (p. 42). Do you agree that people of religious faith are called to serve others even when it involves risk? On pages 43–44, I acknowledge the challenge this poses for me as a Christian. Do you also wrestle with the questions raised on this page?

Chapter 3

If yours is an interfaith group, you may want to start by inviting members from the various religions to flesh out the discussion in this chapter with their own knowledge and experience. If your group does not include Bahá'í, Buddhist, Hindu, Muslim, or Sikh members, this would be the obvious time to invite a speaker/participant from one or more of those traditions.

1. What might your own religious community learn about dealing with fear from one or more of these other religions? Where do you see common ground?

2. Does the idea of holding fear and hope in equilibrium ring true for you? Are there times when it is appropriate to emphasize one more than the other?

3. Discuss the idea that fearing things that are an inevitable part of our impermanent existence, including separation and death, leads only to unhappiness and suffering.
4. How do you respond to the idea that fear may lose its hold on our lives if we are able to look deeply at (meditate on) the things that scare us?

Members of your group might encourage one another to try beginning each day with Gandhi's resolve ("I shall not fear anyone on earth; I shall fear only God") or with the injunction from the Sikh tradition ("I will fear no one and make no one afraid").

Chapter 4

1. If members of your group have traveled to or lived in Israel or the Palestinian territories, ask them about their experience. Were they ever afraid? How present was the concern for security? Again, a visiting speaker who is particularly familiar with the Middle East may be a very useful addition to your conversation.
2. What lessons does this chapter hold for the United States?
3. Authors quoted in this chapter suggest that an obsession with security has led Israel to rationalize practices that run counter to its stated commitment to human rights for all (pp. 66–72). Does this critique also apply to the United States?
4. Discuss the distinction, made on pages 70–71, between physical and symbolic threats. Give examples of each from your own experience.
5. What do you think of the argument (p. 73) that fear can affect the kind of information people choose to receive?
6. The discussion of the Separation Barrier built by Israel (p. 75) relates directly to the discussion of human interdependence in chapters 2 and 3. Studies suggest that separation increases our fear of the unknown "other" and makes it far harder "to differentiate" one's opponents (i.e., to recognize that "they" include individuals with a myriad of backgrounds and opinions). Talk

about the importance of this claim and its implications for America.

Chapter 5

The focus for discussion of this chapter will likely be the ten recommendations (pp. 85–94). Will it be possible for your local community to act on one or more of them? There may also be time for particular questions stemming from the chapter as a whole:

1. How can a community, or a family, find the right balance between safety and hospitality?
2. Does your religious community often live anxiously, unwilling to risk bold witness for fear of losing members or resources? Do you agree that "the level of anxiety in a religious community may well be an indication of its need for renewal, just as an emphasis on human interdependence, along with a refusal to find security in things other than the Divine, is a sign of vitality and health" (p. 84)?
3. Is there reason for people of religious faith to be hopeful? You may want to look back to the final pages of chapter 1 during this discussion. What do you imagine U.S. society will look like in thirty years? What role can religious communities play in bringing about a less fearful future?

Abbreviated Lists of Questions

For an Interfaith Group

1. Do you agree that there is a "culture of fear" in contemporary America? If so, how have you or your religious community experienced it? Which issues in chapter 1 have received particular attention in your community?
2. Three possible explanations for the current prevalence of fear in US public life are named in chapter 1. Which, if any, of these do you find most convincing?
3. What can your religious community learn from other

religions about dealing with fear? What do you see as the common themes running throughout chapters 2 and 3?

4. Do you agree that religions have often used fear in negative ways? How does your community deal with or relate to the fundamentalist strand in your own tradition?
5. Which of the recommendations in chapter 5 seem most important? Which seem most likely to be accomplished? Is it possible for our religious communities to address "deep cultural currents," including fear, together?
6. Is there reason for people of religious faith to be hopeful? How important is it for interfaith partners to express hope together?

For a Christian Group

The questions in the previous list are certainly appropriate for a group made up entirely of Christians. Such a group may want, as well, to reflect on the following (drawn from chapter 2):

1. Chapter 2 identifies a number of biblical passages that you may want to look at more closely, including Psalm 23, Matthew 14:25–31, and Luke 12:16–34. What other parts of Scripture can you think of that speak to the issue of fear? Are there hymns or parts of the liturgy that deal with fear and fearlessness?
2. What does "fear of the Lord" mean to you? Discuss Rabbi Steinberg's statement (p. 31): "Awe is what happens to fear when it stops being about me."
3. Discuss the contention of Thomas Aquinas that fear is "disordered" when we are afraid of things that aren't immediately threatening and when we fear the loss of things that shouldn't be loved (pp. 33–34). Have your fears ever kept you from doing something good for yourself or others?
4. Read together the following assertions:
   – "Christ has borne the anxiety of the world so as to give to the world instead that which is his: his joy, his peace" (Hans Urs von Balthasar, p. 37).

— The only antidote to obsessive fear is the assurance we are loved by a God who sends us to love even those sick with "the poisonous disease of fear" (paraphrasing Martin Luther King Jr., p. 44). Does faith in Christ help you live less fearfully? Does the assurance of God's love put fear in proper perspective?

5. How do you respond to the claim of the United Methodist bishops that "following Jesus leads to radical insecurity" (p. 42)? Most of us, I suspect, want to take our faith seriously, even though it may involve risk (welcoming strangers, giving away personal resources, standing up for Christian values even when it isn't popular); at the same time, we want to have some measure of security for ourselves and those we love most dearly. How do you balance these things in your life? Has the nation gotten "out of balance" in its desire for safety?

Notes

Introduction

1. This was widely reported. See, e.g., "Congressman: Muslims 'Enemy amongst Us,'" WorldNetDaily.com, February 13, 2004, http://www.wnd.com/2004/02/23257/.
2. Quoted in Nihad Awad, "King's Attack on U.S. Muslims: Head of CAIR Says Terrorism Hearings Will Stoke Fears," *New York Daily News*, February 28, 2011, http://www.nydailynews.com/opinion/king-attack-u-s-muslims-head-cair-terrorism-hearings-stoke-fears-article-1.139303.
3. David Schanzer, Charles Kurzman, and Ebrahim Moosa, "Anti-Terror Lessons of Muslim-Americans," a research project funded by the National Institute of Justice and administered by Duke University and the University of North Carolina, January 6, 2010, https://www.ncjrs.gov/pdffiles1/nij/grants/229868.pdf.
4. See Martha C. Nussbaum, *The New Religious Intolerance: Overcoming the Politics of Fear in an Anxious Age* (Cambridge, MA: Belknap Press, 2012), 43–48. Chapter 2 of Nussbaum's book is an incisive discussion of fear as a narcissistic emotion.
5. "Remarks by the President at National Prayer Breakfast," February 4, 2016, https://www.whitehouse.gov/the-press-office/2016/02/04/remarks-president-national-prayer-breakfast-0.
6. Martin Luther King Jr., "Antidotes for Fear," in *The Essential Writings and Speeches of Martin Luther King, Jr.*, ed. James M. Washington (San Francisco: HarperCollins, 1991), 511.
7. Ta-Nehisi Coates, *Between the World and Me* (New York: Spiegel & Grau, 2015), 17.
8. Ibid., 16–17.
9. Bureau of Justice Statistics, "Homicide Trends in the United States," http://www.bjs.gov/content/pub/pdf/htius.pdf. See also Firmin DeBrabander, *Do Guns Make Us Free?: Democracy and the Armed Society* (New Haven, CT: Yale University Press, 2015), 24–25.
10. Coates, *Between*, 28.

11. Bertrand Russell, "Why I Am Not a Christian" (lecture, Battersea Town Hall, London, March 6, 1927), http://www.users.drew.edu/~jlenz/whynot.html.
12. For a discussion of violence done in the name of religion in our era, see Charles Kimball, *When Religion Becomes Lethal* (San Francisco: Jossey-Bass, 2011); and Mark Jurgensmeyer, *Terror in the Mind of God* (Berkeley: University of California Press, 2000).
13. Pew Research Center, "The Torture Debate: A Closer Look," May 7, 2009, http://www.pewforum.org/2009/05/07/the-torture-debate-a-closer-look/.
14. Paul Tillich, *The Courage to Be* (New Haven, CT: Yale University Press, 1952), 39.
15. Dominique Moïsi, *The Geopolitics of Emotion* (New York: Anchor Books, 2009), 108.

Chapter 1: The Culture of Fear in Contemporary America
1. "Gov. Greg Abbott Says Texas Will Not Accept Any Syrian Refugees," http://abc13.com/news/texas-governor-says-state-will-not-accept-syrian-refugees/1086456/.
2. Quoted in Michelle Ye Hee Lee, "Fact Checker: The viral claim that 'not one' refugee resettled since 9/11 has been 'arrested on domestic terrorism charges,'" *Washington Post*, November 19, 2015, https://www.washingtonpost.com/news/fact-checker/wp/2015/11/19/the-viral-claim-that-not-one-refugee-resettled-since-911-has-been-arrested-on-domestic-terrorism-charges/.
3. Seth G. Jones, "The Terrorism Threat to the United States and Implications for Refugees," RAND Corporation, June 2015, http://www.rand.org/content/dam/rand/pubs/testimonies/CT400/CT433/RAND_CT433.pdf.
4. "The Price of Fear," *New York Times*, November 20, 2015, http://www.nytimes.com/2015/11/21/opinion/the-price-of-fear.html?_r=0.
5. Quoted in Cary Gibson, "Meeting Hatred with Unity," *U.S. News and World Report*, November 24, 2015, http://www.usnews.com/opinion/blogs/opinion-blog/2015/11/24/we-mustnt-let-our-response-to-paris-reinforce-terrorists-hatred-and-fear.
6. Romain Gonzalez, "A French Psychoanalyst Talks about Fear, Anxiety, and the Paris Attacks," *VICE*, November 15, 2015, http://www.vice.com/read/helene-lheuillet-interview-how-to-control-fear-876 .
7. Cornel West once observed that 9/11 was "the first time that many Americans of various colors felt unsafe"—a feeing, he noted, that has been all too familiar for African Americans (quoted in Ryan Herring, "When Terror Wears a Badge," http://sojo.net/blogs/2014/08/14/when-terror-wears-badge).
8. David Rothkopf, "Scared Tactics," *Foreign Policy*, June 19, 2013, http://foreignpolicy.com/2013/06/19/scared-tactics/.
9. David Rothkopf, "Declaring an End to the Decade of Fear," *Foreign Policy*, August 1, 2013, http://www.foreignpolicy.com/articles/2013/08/01/declaring_an_end_to_the_decade_of_fear
10. See Peter N. Stearns, "Fear and History," http://www.nnet.gr/historein/historeinfiles/histvolumes/hist08/historein8-stearns.pdf, 19–20.
11. Ibid., 20.

12. "Deadly Attacks since 9/11," The International Security Program (New America), http://securitydata.newamerica.net/extremists/deadly-attacks.html.

13. Scott Shane, "Homegrown Extremists Tied to Deadlier Toll than Jihadists in U.S. since 9/11," New York Times, June 24, 2015, http://www.nytimes.com/2015/06/25/us/tally-of-attacks-in-us-challenges-perceptions-of-top-terror-threat.html.

14. Brad Plumer, "Eight Facts about Terrorism in the United States," Washington Post, April 16, 2013, https://www.washingtonpost.com/news/wonk/wp/2013/04/16/eight-facts-about-terrorism-in-the-united-states/.

15. Gallup, "Terrorism in the United States," http://www.gallup.com/poll/4909/terrorism-united-states.aspx. The 49 percent figure comes from the June 2015 survey.

16. This comes from the National Priorities Project report of May 26, 2011, https://www.nationalpriorities.org/analysis/2011/us-security-spending-since-911/.

17. This information is widely available. See, e.g., "The United States Spends More on Defense than the Next Seven Countries Combined," Peter G. Peterson Foundation, April 18, 2016, http://pgpf.org/Chart-Archive/0053_defense-comparison.

18. Cited in Timothy Egan, "What to Be Afraid Of," New York Times, June 5, 2015, http://www.nytimes.com/2015/06/05/opinion/what-to-be-afraid-of.html.

19. Fareed Zakaria, The Post-American World (New York: W. W. Norton & Co., 2008), 251.

20. Ibid., 48.

21. James Traub, "When Did America Give Up on the Idea of America?," Foreign Policy, December 9, 2015, http://foreignpolicy.com/2015/12/09/when-did-america-give-up-on-the-idea-of-america/.

22. Ibid.

23. Barry Glassner, The Culture of Fear: Why Americans Are Afraid of the Wrong Things, Tenth Anniversary Edition (New York: Basic Books, 1999), esp. chaps. 1 and 2.

24. Federal Bureau of Investigation, "Crime in the United States 2014," https://ucr.fbi.gov/crime-in-the-u.s/2014/crime-in-the-u.s.-2014/offenses-known-to-law-enforcement/violent-crime. See also David K. Sutton, "U.S. Crime Rates 1960–2010: The Facts Might Surprise You," The Left Call, February 23, 2012, http://leftcall.com/4557/u-s-crime-rates-1960-2010-the-facts-might-surprise-you/.

25. A study conducted by the Brennan Center for Justice at NYU found that, despite an increase in the number of murders in certain cities, overall crime still declined in 2015. See Harry Bruinius, "In the United States, Anxiety Is Up, but Crime Is Down," Christian Science Monitor, December 28, 2015, http://www.csmonitor.com/USA/Justice/2015/1228/In-the-United-States-anxiety-is-up-but-crime-is-down.

26. Lydia Saad, "Most Americans Believe Crime in U.S. Is Worsening," October 31, 2011, http://www.gallup.com/poll/150464/americans-believe-crime-worsening.aspx.

27. Statistics on incarceration rates are widely available. See, e.g., http://www.nytimes.com/2008/04/23/world/americas/23iht-23prison.12253738.html?pagewanted=all.

28. Christopher Ingraham, "The States That Spend More Money on Prisoners Than College Students," *Washington Post*, July 7, 2016, http://www.standard.net/National/2016/07/07/The-states-that-spend-more-money-on-prisoners-than-college-students.

29. Mona Chalabi, "Gun Homicides and Gun Ownership Listed by Country" (Datablog), *The Guardian*, July 22, 2012, https://www.theguardian.com/news/datablog/2012/jul/22/gun-homicides-ownership-world-list.

30. Cited in Firmin DeBrabander, *Do Guns Make Us Free? Democracy and the Armed Society* (New Haven, CT: Yale University Press, 2015), 17.

31. Ibid., xiv.

32. Bryan Massingale, "When Profiling Is 'Reasonable,' Injustice Becomes Excusable," *U.S. Catholic* (blog), http://www.uscatholic.org/blog/201307/when-profiling-"reasonable"-injustice-becomes-excusable-27574.

33. Alexandra Petri, "The Scariest Thing about Trayvon Martin," *Washington Post*, March 24, 2012, http://www.washingtonpost.com/blogs/compost/post/the-scariest-thing-about-trayvon-martin/2012/03/20/gIQAfKlLSS_blog.html.

34. "Dallas Dad's Message for Cops: Don't Be Afraid of Black Men," NBC Nightly News, July 8, 2016, http://www.nbcnews.com/nightly-news/video/dallas-dad-s-message-for-cops-don-t-be-afraid-of-black-men-721547331709.

35. Frank Furedi, NY Salon speaker paper, http://www.nysalon.org/event_speakerpapers/Furedi.pdf.

36. Brady Dennis and Peyton M. Craighill, "Ebola Poll: Two-Thirds of Americans Worried about Possible Widespread Epidemic in U.S.," *Washington Post*, October 14, 2014, https://www.washingtonpost.com/national/health-science/ebola-poll-two-thirds-of-americans-worried-about-possible-widespread-epidemic-in-us/2014/10/13/d0afd0ee-52ff-11e4-809b-8cc0a295c773_story.html.

37. Stearns, "Fear and History," 17.

38. Quoted in Wyatt Mason, "The Revelations of Marilynne Robinson," *New York Times Magazine*, October 1, 2014, http://www.nytimes.com/2014/10/05/magazine/the-revelations-of-marilynne-robinson.html?_r=0.

39. Quoted by President Obama during his presentation to the 2016 National Prayer Breakfast, https://www.whitehouse.gov/the-press-office/2016/02/04/remarks-president-national-prayer-breakfast-0.

40. Stearns, "Fear and History," 21.

41. Peter N. Stearns, *American Fear: The Causes and Consequences of High Anxiety* (New York and London: Routledge, 2006), 19.

42. Möisi, *Geopolitics*, 91.

43. Ibid., 90. This is reinforced by Kenneth Roth, executive director of Human Rights Watch, who begins the group's 2016 world report by arguing that "fear stood behind many of the big human rights developments of the past year," including fear of what an influx of asylum seekers might mean for Western societies. Available at https://www.hrw.org/world-report/2016.

44. Tony Judt, *Ill Fares the Land* (London: Penquin Books, 2010), 217.

45. Cliff Young and Chris Jackson, "The Rise of Neo-Nativism: Putting Trump into Proper Context," Ipsos Ideas Spotlight, October 9, 2015, http://spotlight

.ipsos-na.com/index.php/news/the-rise-of-neo-nativism-putting-trump-into -proper-context/.

46. Michael Gerson, "Republicans Are Still in Denial over Donald Trump," Washington Post Writers Group, November 26, 2015, http://www.alipac .us/f9/michael-gerson-republicans-still-denial-over-donald-trump-325716/. If these perceptions need further corroboration, it is provided by a Public Religion Research Institute–Brookings survey that found that seven in ten white evangelical Protestants believe the United States has changed for the worse since the 1950s. See Robert P. Jones, "The Evangelicals and the Great Trump Hope," *New York Times*, July 11, 2016, http://www.nytimes.com/2016/07/11 /opinion/campaign-stops/the-evangelicals-and-the-great-trump-hope.html. Jones's new book on this subject is *The End of White Christian America* (New York: Simon & Schuster, 2016).

47. The mayor of Murrieta, who led the protests, linked the opposition to a fear of disease. See Jeremy Adam Smith, "Our Fear of Immigrants," *Pacific Standard*, July 23, 2014, https://psmag.com/our-fear-of-immigrants-c29a882bbc5a# .vffxdxt4o.

48. Jim Wallis, "The Moral Failure of Immigration Reform: Are We Really Afraid of Children?," *Sojourners*, July 3, 2014, http://sojo.net/blogs/2014/07/03 /moral-failure-immigration-reform-are-we-really-afraid-children.

49. Frank Furedi, "The Only Thing We Have to Fear Is the 'Culture of Fear' Itself," *Spiked*, April 4, 2007, http://frankfuredi.com/pdf/fearessay-20070404.pdf.

50. See Frank Furedi, *The Politics of Fear: Beyond Left and Right* (London: Continuum Press, 2006).

51. Glassner, *Culture of Fear*, xxxvi.

52. Ibid., xxix.

53. Quoted in DeBrabander, *Do Guns*, 20.

54. Leonard Pitts, "With Gun Violence, Fact Is No Match for Fear," *Seattle Times*, November 8, 2015, http://www.seattletimes.com/opinion/with-gun-violence -fact-is-no-match-for-fear/.

55. NRA, "Demons at Our Door," https://www.nranews.com/series/freedoms -safest-place/video/freedoms-safest-place-demons-at-our-door/episode /freedoms-safest-place-season-1-episode-9-demons-at-our-door.

56. The quotations are from a Media Matters Action Network Study, "Fear and Loathing in Prime Time: Immigration Myths and Cable News," http:// mediamattersaction.org/reports/fearandloathing/.

57. Cited in ibid.

58. See Eduardo Porter, "Illegal Immigrants and Bolstering Social Security with Billions," *New York Times*, April 5, 2005, http://www.nytimes .com/2005/04/05/business/illegal-immigrants-are-bolstering-social-security -with-billions.html.

59. This topic is thoroughly explored in Corey Robin, *Fear: The History of a Political Idea* (Oxford: Oxford University Press, 2004).

60. David Remnick, "Stranger than Fiction," *New Yorker*, October 26, 2015, http://www.newyorker.com/magazine/2015/10/26/stranger-than-fiction-a -turning-point-for-hillary-clinton.

61. Quoted in a *New York Times* review of Robert Mann, *A Grand Delusion*, https://www.nytimes.com/books/first/m/mann-delusion.html.
62. See Daniel Gardner, *The Science of Fear* (New York: Plume Book, 2009), 267.
63. See *The Millennium Development Goals Report 2013*, http://www.un.org /millenniumgoals/pdf/report-2013/mdg-report-2013-english.pdf. See also Steven Radelet, "The War against Global Poverty: How We're Winning," *Christian Science Monitor Weekly*, February 8, 2016, 28–32.
64. See Steven Pinker, *The Better Angels of Our Nature: Why Violence Has Declined* (London: Penguin, 2011), chap. 3.
65. See Nicholas Kristof, "Scrooges of the World, Begone!," *New York Times*, December 24, 2014, http://www.nytimes.com/2014/12/25/opinion/nicholas -kristof-scrooges-of-the-world-begone.html.
66. Michael Gerson, "The Golden Age of Aid," *Washington Post*, September 29, 2015, https://www.washingtonpost.com/opinions/wiping-out-malaria-in-a -generation/2015/09/28/7e281310-6607-11e5-8325-a42b5a459b1e_story.html.
67. This is from a report by the Barna Group. See "Global Poverty Is on the Decline, but Almost No One Believes It," https://www.barna.org /barna-update/culture/668-global-poverty-is-on-the-decline-but-almost-no -one-believes-it#.V5_QY0tM4y7.
68. Gardner, *Science of Fear*, 10.
69. Danny Westneat, "2014 Is One Year in Need of an Image Makeover," *Seattle Times*, December 27, 2014, http://www.seattletimes.com/seattle-news /2014-is-one-year-in-need-of-an-image-makeover/.
70. The statements are from 2016 Republican presidential candidates Donald Trump, Ted Cruz, Ben Carson, and Chris Christie.

Chapter 2: Jewish and Christian Responses to Fear

1. Scott Bader-Saye, "Thomas Aquinas and the Culture of Fear," *Journal of the Society of Christian Ethics* 25, 2 (2005): 106.
2. See Corey Robin, *Fear: The History of a Political Idea* (Oxford: Oxford University Press, 2004), 7.
3. Babylonian Talmud: Tractate Berakhot, 61b.
4. Ibid., 33b. A good resource for such materials is C. G. Montefiore and H. Loewe, *A Rabbinic Anthology* (New York: Schocken Books, 1974).
5. Toba Spitzer, "Asking for Fear," http://dorsheitzedek.org/writings/asking-for -fear.
6. The quotation is that of a nineteenth-century Russian Hasidic rabbi, Aaron of Karlin II. It is quoted in Martin Buber, *Tales of the Hasidim: Early Masters* (New York: Schocken Books, 1947), 25.
7. Quoted by Yael Splansky, "Fear Not" (D'var Torah commentary), *ReformJudaism .org*, August 19, 2012, http://blogs.rj.org/blog/2012/08/19/dvar-torah-fear -not/.
8. Simeon ben Eleazar: "Greater is he who acts from love than he who acts from fear" (Babylonian Talmud: Tractate Sotah, 31a).
9. Abraham Joshua Heschel, *God in Search of Man* (New York: Harper & Row, 1955), 77.

10. Ibid., 74.
11. Quoted in Spitzer, "Asking for Fear."
12. The problem, writes Scott Bader-Saye, is not in having savings; good steward-ship and delayed gratification are virtues. It is a problem when "we can no lon-ger make good judgments about what is enough" (Scott Bader-Saye, *Following Jesus in a Culture of Fear* [Grand Rapids: Brazos Press, 2007], 135).
13. Various renditions of this folk song are accessible online. See, e.g., https://www.youtube.com/watch?v=GusLcXuVOJI. The song became very popular in Israel during the 1973 Yom Kippur War, a time of great national danger.
14. David Brooks, "On Conquering Fear," *New York Times*, April 3, 2015, http://www.nytimes.com/2015/04/03/opinion/david-brooks-on-conquering-fear.html?_r=0.
15. Aquinas's treatment of the subject is found in his *Summa Theologica*, part 2. This portion of the *Summa* is, itself, divided into two parts. The discussion of fear is in the first part of part 2 (1-2), qq. 41–44, and the second part of part 2 (2-2), qq. 19, 22, 125–27. An excellent commentary on Aquinas's under-standing of fear, one to which I am indebted, is provided by Scott Bader-Saye. In addition to Bader-Saye, "Thomas Aquinas and the Culture of Fear," see Bader-Saye, *Following Jesus*, chaps. 2–4.
16. See Barry Glassner, *The Culture of Fear: Why Americans Are Afraid of the Wrong Things*, Tenth Anniversary Edition (New York: Basic Books, 1999), 44–45.
17. Bader-Saye, "Thomas Aquinas and the Culture of Fear," 103–4.
18. Aquinas, *Summa* 2-2, q. 19, a. 3.
19. Bader-Saye, "Thomas Aquinas and the Culture of Fear," 104.
20. Aristotle, *Nicomachean Ethics*, book 3, chap. 7.
21. Aquinas, *Summa*, 2-2, q. 126, a. 2. See Bader-Saye, "Thomas Aquinas and the Culture of Fear," 105.
22. Ibid., 1-2, q. 44, a. 1.
23. Søren Kierkegaard, *The Concept of Anxiety*, trans. Alastair Hannay (New York: W. W. Norton & Co., 2014). Kierkegaard's work was originally published in English, translated by Walter Lowrie, as *The Concept of Dread*. For a popular look at Kierkegaard and anxiety, see Gordon Marino, "The Danish Doctor of Dread," *New York Times*, March 17, 2012, http://opinionator.blogs.nytimes.com/2012/03/17/the-danish-doctor-of-dread/.
24. Arthur M. Schlesinger Jr., *The Vital Center: The Politics of Freedom* (New Brunswick, NJ: Transaction Publishers, 1998), 1.
25. Hans Urs von Balthasar, *The Christian and Anxiety*, trans. Dennis D. Martin and Michael J. Miller (San Francisco: Ignatius Press, 2000), 35–36.
26. Ibid., 81 and 88.
27. Ibid., 88.
28. Paul Tillich, *The Courage to Be* (New Haven, CT: Yale University Press, 1952), 112. The types of anxiety discussed in the previous paragraphs are presented on pages 40–63.
29. Ibid., 49–50.
30. Ibid., 76.

31. Ibid., 62.
32. Ibid.
33. Ibid., 39.
34. Bader-Saye, *Following Jesus*, 105.
35. See Tillich, *Courage*, 75.
36. Ibid., 186ff.
37. Ibid., 141.
38. *In Search of Security*, published by the United Methodist Council of Bishops Task Force on Safety and Security, 9.
39. Ibid., 11.
40. Ibid.
41. Marilynne Robinson, "Fear," *New York Review of Books*, September 24, 2015, 28.
42. *In Search*, 15.
43. Ibid., 25.
44. See Bader-Saye, *Following Jesus*, 29.
45. Martin Luther King Jr., "Draft of Chapter XIV: 'The Mastery of Fear or Antidotes for Fear,'" in Clayborne Carson, ed., *The Papers of Martin Luther King, Jr.*, vol. 6 (Berkeley: University of California Press, 2007), 540–41. A revised version of this sermon became chapter 14 in King's collection of sermons *Strength to Love*.
46. King, "Draft of Chapter XIV," 536.
47. Ibid., 544.
48. Marilyn Chandler McEntyre, "An Invitation to Insecurity," *Weavings* 21, 5 (2006): 13.
49. Martin Luther King Jr., "A Christmas Sermon on Peace," in James M. Washington, ed., *A Testament of Hope: The Essential Writings and Speeches of Martin Luther King, Jr.* (New York: HarperCollins, 1986), 254.
50. Ami Ayalon, "Israel's Response Is Proportionate to Hamas's Threat," *New York Times*, July 23, 2014, http://nytimes.com/roomfordebate/2014/07/22/self-defense-or-atrocties-in-gaza/israels-response-is-proportionate-to-hamass-threat.
51. The numbers are easily accessible. See, e.g., "Defense Spending vs. International Aid: It's a Big Difference," The Borgen Project, http://borgenproject.org/defense-spending-vs-international-aid-big-difference/.
52. I have heard this point made by Jim Wallis, founder and editor of *Sojourners* magazine.

Chapter 3: The Response of Other Religions to Fear

1. The Bahá'í sacred texts are available from the Bahá'í Reference Library online. See http://reference.bahai.org/en/t/b/GWB/gwb-128.html.
2. Bahá'í Reference Library, http://reference.bahai.org/en/t/b/TB/tb-9.html.
3. Quoted in Matt Giani, "The Fear of God. What Does It Mean?" (blog), bahaiblog.net/site 2012/09/the-fear-of-god-what-does-it-mean/, accessed May 3, 2016. Several Bahá'í teachings regarding fear can be found in *Lights of Guidance*, section 18, http://bahai-library.com/hornby_lights_guidance.

4. Dale E. Lehman, "Freedom from Fear," Planet Bahá'í, September 13, 2002, http://www.planetbahai.org/cgi-bin/articles.pl?article=111&print=Y.

5. Bahá'í Reference Library, http://reference.bahai.org/en/t/b/SVFV/svfv-12.html.

6. See "Guru Nanak's Challenge to Terrorism," http://www.gurmat.info/sms/smsarticles/advisorypanel/gurmukhsinghsewauk/gurunanakschallengetoterrorism.html.

7. A search engine for the Guru Granth Sahib is available at http://www.srigranth.org/servlet/gurbani.gurbani?S=y. These quotations are Guru Granth Sahib, p. 54, line 18, and p. 18, line 6.

8. Guru Granth Sahib, p. 293, line 8.

9. "Guru Nanak's Challenge to Terrorism."

10. Guru Granth Sahib, p. 1427, line 7.

11. Abu Hamid Muhammed al-Ghazali, The Book of Fear and Hope, trans. William McKane (Leiden: E. J. Brill, 1965), xiv, xi.

12. Ibid., 29.

13. Ibid., 48.

14. Quoted in ibid., 10.

15. Ibid., 55; see also p. 41.

16. Ibn ul Qayyim al-Jawziyyah, "The Station of Fear," http://www.ummah.com/forum/showthread.php?112727-The-Station-of-Fear!&s=2c51dff7bceff57aca50441c02deae29.

17. Ibid.This image is in the appendix to the basic text, titled "Balancing Fear with Hope."

18. Sayyid Mujtaba Musavi Lari, "Chapter 14: 'Fear,'" Ethics and Spiritual Growth, trans. Ali Quli Qara'i (Qum: Ansariym Publications, 1997). Accessed online at https://www.al-islam.org/ethics-and-spiritual-growth-sayyid-mujtaba-musawi-lari/chapter-14-fear. There are no page numbers in the version online.

19. Ibid.

20. Ibid.

21. Ibid.

22. A good brief discussion of the Arabic words for fear found in the Qur'an is in al-Jawziyyah, "The Station of Fear." See also Amatullah, "Usage of 'Fear' in the Qur'an," April 18, 2009 (blog), https://tayyibaat.wordpress.com/2009/04/18/usage-of-fear-in-the-quran/. The English translation of the Qur'an is from The Study Quran: A New Translation and Commentary, ed., Seyyed Hossein Nasr (New York: HarperOne, 2015).

23. Quoted in Abbas al-Qummi, "The Stages of the Hereafter," http://islamicblessings.com/upload/Stages of the Hereafter.pdf. This is an online version of Sheik al-Qummi's well-known treatise.

24. See Qur'an 20:45, 26:14, and 11:69–70.

25. A good discussion of this material is Hafsa Kanjwal, "Response to Fear in the Muslim Tradition," Interreligious Dialogue, http://irdialogue.org/wp-content/uploads/2010/12/Response-to-Fear-in-the-Muslim-Tradition-by-Hafsa-Kanjwal-.pdf.

26. Council on American-Islamic Relations, *Confronting Fear: Islamophobia and Its Impact in the U.S. 2013–2015*, updated June 20, 2016, http://www.islamophobia.org/15-reports/179-confronting-fear-islamophobia-and-its-impact-in-the-u-s-2013-2015.html.

27. See Kevin Sullivan, Elahe Izadi, and Sarah Pulliam Bailey, "After Paris and California Attacks, U.S. Muslims Feel Intense Backlash," *Washington Post*, December 3, 2015, https://www.washingtonpost.com/national/after-paris-and-california-attacks-us-muslims-feel-intense-backlash/2015/12/03/bcf8e480-9a09-11e5-94f0-9eeaff906ef3_story.html.

28. See Shantideva, *Bodhisattvacharyavatara*, "A Guide to a Bodhisattva's Way of Life," chap. 5, verse 8, http://www.abuddhistlibrary.com/Buddhism/A%20-%20Tibetan%20Buddhism/Authors/Shantideva/A%20Guide%20to%20the%20Bodhisattva's%20Way%20of%20Life%20-%20%20Stephen%20Bachelor%20tra/A%20Guide%20to%20the%20Bodhisattva's%20Way%20of%20Life.pdf. The translation quoted is from Mahakankala Buddhist Center, "What is Fear?," http://meditationinsantabarbara.org/dealing-with-fear/.

29. Dhammapada, 212–16, http://viewonbuddhism.org/dharma-quotes-quotations-buddhist/fear-anxiety.htm. See also Dhammapada, 39: "There is no fear for one whose mind is not filled with desires."

30. Thanissaro Bhikkhu, *The Karma of Questions: Essays on the Buddhist Path* (printed by the author, 2002), 25.

31. Pema Chödrön, *The Places That Scare You: A Guide to Fearlessness in Difficult Times* (Boston: Shambhala, 2002), 4.

32. Ibid., 11–15.

33. Ibid., 19.

34. Ibid., 41.

35. Ibid., 6.

36. Thich Nhat Hanh, *Fear: Essential Wisdom for Getting through the Storm* (New York: HarperCollins, 2012), 1, 60.

37. Ibid., 48–51.

38. Ibid., 38.

39. Quoted in Ibid., 57.

40. Ibid., 105–6.

41. Thanissaro, *The Karma*, 25.

42. Ibid., 25.

43. Nhat Hanh, *Fear*, 95–119. For the relationship of fear and society, see also Judith Lief, "Starting on the Path of Fear and Fearlessness," *Lion's Roar*, January 1, 2008. Lief's essay is one of five essays on the topic "Fear and Fearlessness: What the Buddhists Teach." All of them are useful for our study.

44. Aung Sang Suu Kyi, "Freedom from Fear," http://www.thirdworldtraveler.com/Burma/FreedomFromFearSpeech.html. The speech is included in Aung San Suu Kyi, *Freedom from Fear* (London: Penguin, 1991).

45. Ibid.

46. Ibid.

47. Joseph M. Kitagawa, *Religions of the East* (Philadelphia: Westminster Press, 1968), 104.

48. "Swami Vivekananda Quotes on Fear and Fearlessness," http://www
.thespiritualindian.com/swami-vivekananda-quotes-on-fear-and-fearlessness/.

49. Swami Vivekananda, "The Complete Works of Swami Vivekananda/Volume
7/Conversations and Dialogues/V," *Wikisource*, https://en.wikisource
.org/wiki
/The_Complete_Works_of_Swami_Vivekananda/Volume_7/Conversations
_And_Dialogues/V.

50. Swami Vivekananda, "The Complete Works of Swami Vivekananda/Volume 3/
Lectures from Colombo to Almora/Reply to the Address of Welcome at Para-
makudi," *Wikisource*, https://en.wikisource.org/wiki/The_Complete_Works_of
_Swami_Vivekananda/Volume_3/Lectures_from_Colombo_to_Almora/Reply
_to_the_Address_of_Welcome_at_Paramakudi.

51. "Swami Vivekananda Quotes on Fear," December 2, 2013, http://www
.swamivivekanandaquotes.org/2013/12/swami-vivekanandas-quotes-on-fear
.html.

52. Swami Vivekananda, "The Complete Works of Swami Vivekananda/Volume
2/Practical Vedanta and Other Lectures/The Way to Blessedness," https://
en.wikisource.org/wiki/The_Complete_Works_of_Swami_Vivekananda
/Volume_2/The_Powers_of_the_Mind.

53. Isa Upanishad, 6.

54. Vivekananda, "Complete Works of Swami Vivekananda/Volume 2."

55. Vivekananda, "Complete Works of Swami Vivekananda/Volume 7."

56. See "Swami Vivekananda Quotes on Fear and Fearlessness" and Vivekananda,
"Complete Works of Swami Vivekananda/Volume 7."

57. Swami Vivekananda, "The Complete Works of Swami Vivekananda/Volume
6/EpistlesSecond Series/LX Mrs. Bull," *Wikisource*, https://en.wikisource
.org/wiki/The_Complete_Works_of_Swami_Vivekananda/Volume_6
/Epistles_-_Second_Series/LX_Mrs._Bull.

58. Quoted in Uma Majmudar, "Swami Vivekananda and Mahatma Gandhi:
Truth Is One, Paths Are Diverse," *American Vedantist*, americanvedantist
.org/2013/articles/swami-vivekananda-and-mahatma-gandhi-truth-is-one
-paths-are-diverse/. Gandhi is here drawing on language from the Bhagavad-
Gita, chap. 2, verses 71–72.

59. Images for this quotation are available on Pinterest at https://www.pinterest
.com/pin/258675572319372930/.

Chapter 4: The Israeli-Palestinian Conflict: A Case Study

1. Eran Halperin, *Emotions in Conflict: Inhibitors and Facilitators of Peace Making* (New York and London: Routledge, 2016), 67.

2. Ingrid Baukhol, "Security and Fear in Israeli and Palestinian Conflict Narra-
tives" (master's thesis, University of Gothenburg, 2015), 60, https://gupea.ub.gu
.se/bitstream/2077/39985/4/gupea_2077_39985_4.pdf.

3. Dominique Moïsi, *The Geopolitics of Emotion* (New York: Anchor Books,
2009), 56–57.

4. Daniel Bar-Tal, "Why Does Fear Override Hope in Societies Engulfed by
Intractable Conflict, as It Does in the Israeli Society?," *Political Psychology*
22, no. 3 (2001): 621.

5. "Terrorism against Israel: Comprehensive Listing of Fatalities," Jewish Virtual Library, http://www.jewishvirtuallibrary.org/jsource/Terrorism/victims.html.

6. Juliana Ochs, *Security and Suspicion: An Ethnography of Everyday Life in Israel* (Philadelphia: University of Pennsylvania Press, 2011), 2. Ochs is quoting Dorit Beinisch, former president of the Supreme Court of Israel.

7. Ibid., 16 and 76.

8. Quoted in Ibid., 65.

9. Ibid., 65.

10. Ibid., 12.

11. Quoted in Zygmunt Bauman, *Liquid Fear* (Cambridge: Polity Press, 2006), 132. Altheide's essay "Mass Media, Crime, and the Discourse of Fear" appears in the Fall 2003 issue of *Hedgehog Review*, which includes several helpful essays on the topic.

12. Ibid., 3–4.

13. Eran Halperin, Neta Oren, and Daniel Bar-Tal, "Socio-Psychological Barriers to Resolving the Israeli-Palestinian Conflict: An Analysis of Jewish Israeli Society," in *Barriers to Peace in the Israeli-Palestinian Conflict*, ed. Yaacov Bar-Siman-Tov, published by the Konrad-Adenauer-Stiftung Israel and the Jerusalem Institute for Israeli Studies, 2010, 45. The volume is available online at http://www.kas.de/wf/doc/kas_22213-1522-2-30.pdf?110316110504.

14. Boaz Yakin, "Israel Is Not Afraid. Israel Is Comfortable," *Huffington Post*, May 26, 2015, http://www.huffingtonpost.com/boaz-yakin/israel-is-not-afraid-isra_b_6943754.html.

15. Halperin, *Emotions in Conflict*, 74.

16. Quoted in Bar-Tal, "Why Does Fear Override Hope," 612.

17. Quoted in Halperin, Oren, and Bar-Tal, "Socio-Psychological Barriers," 39.

18. Quoted in "Ya'alon Pans Netanyahu as Fear-Monger, Announces Run in Next Election," *Jerusalem Post*, August 3, 2016, http://www.jpost.com/Israel-News/Yaalon-Israel-doesnt-face-any-existential-threat-not-even-Iran-456978.

19. Quoted in John Reed, "Israeli Former Defence Chiefs Hit at PM Benjamin Netanyahu," *Financial Times*, June 17, 2016, https://next.ft.com/content/a5480992-3478-11e6-bda0-04585c31b153.

20. Quoted in ibid. See also Ari Shavit, "Is Israel Losing Its Soul?," *Politico*, March 20, 2015. Shavit is the author of the widely acclaimed *My Promised Land: The Triumph and Tragedy of Israel*.

21. Halperin, *Emotions in Conflict*, 81.

22. Ibid., 80.

23. Halperin, Oren, and Bar-Tal, "Socio-Psychological Barriers," 34. On how fear "freezes beliefs," see Daniel Bar-Tal, "Psychological Obstacles to Peace-Making in the Middle East and Proposals to Overcome Them," *Conflict and Communication Online* 4, 1 (2005): 5, http://www.cco.regener-online.de/2005_1/pdf_2005_1/bar_tal.pdf.

24. See Nimrod Rosler, "Fear and Conflict Resolution: Theoretical Discussion and a Case Study from Israel," University of Maryland Institute for Israel Studies,

November 2013, 8. It is accessible at http://israelstudies.umd.edu/files/Nimrod Rosler Research Paper - Nov. 2013.pdf.

25. Halperin, *Emotions in Conflict*, 78.

26. Ibid., 4, 70.

27. Halperin, Oren, and Bar-Tal, "Socio-Psychological Barriers," 42.

28. Halperin, *Emotions in Conflict*, 73.

29. See Bar-Tal, "Psychological Obstacles," 5; Halperin, *Emotions in Conflict*, 79.

30. Yitzak Reiter, "Religion as a Barrier to Compromise in the Israeli-Palestinian Conflict," in Bar-Simon-Tov, ed., *Barriers to Peace*.

31. Zachary K. Rothschild, Abdolhossein Abdollahi, and Tom Psyzczynski, "Does Peace Have a Prayer?," *Journal of Experimental Social Psychology* 45 (2009): 816–27.

32. Quoted in Ochs, *Security and Suspicion*, 140.

33. Ethan Bronner, "A Damaging Distance," *New York Times*, July 13, 2014, http://www.nytimes.com/2014/07/13/sunday-review/for-israelis-and-palestinians -separation-is-dehumanizing.html?_r=0.

34. Martin Luther King Jr., "Advice for Living," The Martin Luther King, Jr. Papers Project, http://okra.stanford.edu/transcription/document_images/Vol04Scans /401_May-1958_Advice for Living.pdf.

35. Christa Case Bryant, "Barriers between Israel and Palestinian Territory Also Block Relationships," *Christian Century*, January 21, 2015, 14.

36. Bernard Avishai et al., "Israel and Palestine: Where to Go from Here," *Harper's*, September 2014.

37. Quoted in Case Bryant, "Barriers between Israel and Palestinian Territory," 14.

38. Halperin, Oren, and Bar-Tal, "Socio-Psychological Barriers," 35.

39. Cited in ibid., 36.

40. Bar-Tal, "Psychological Obstacles," 9.

41. Roger Cohen, "Will the Voices of Conscience Be Heard?," *New York Times*, August 9, 2014, http://www.handinhandk12.org/news/roger-cohen-aug-2014.

42. Juliana Schroeder and Jane L. Risen, "Peace through Friendship," *New York Times*, August 22, 2014, http://www.nytimes.com/2014/08/24/opinion/sunday /peace-through-friendship.html?_r=0.

43. "Charter on Uprooting Hatred and Terror," http://www.seedsofpeace.org /our-values/charter-on-uprooting-hatred-and-terror/.

44. Moïsi, *Geopolitics of Emotion*, 96.

45. David Grossman, "How Fear Kills the Soul," *The Age*, September 27, 2001, http://www.thirdworldtraveler.com/Sept_11_2001/How_Fear_Kills_Soul .html.

Chapter 5: Recommendations for Religious Communities

1. For a discussion of fear and narcissism, see Martha C. Nussbaum, *The New Religious Intolerance: Overcoming the Politics of Fear in an Anxious Age* (Cambridge, MA: Belknap Press, 2012), 55–58.

2. Corey Robin, *Fear: The History of a Political Idea* (Oxford: Oxford University Press, 2004), 251–52.

3. Scott Bader-Saye, *Following Jesus in a Culture of Fear* (Grand Rapids: Brazos Press, 2007), 71–72.

4. I have published two sets of guidelines for having difficult conversations. A list growing out of my work in ecumenical settings is in Michael Kinnamon, *Truth and Community: Diversity and Its Limits in the Ecumenical Movement* (Grand Rapids: Eerdmans, 1988), 29–32. A list focused specifically on maintaining Jewish-Christian relations when disagreeing about the Israeli-Palestinian conflict is in Michael Kinnamon, *Can a Renewal Movement Be Renewed?: Questions for the Future of Ecumenism* (Grand Rapids: Eerdmans, 2014), 112–20.

5. Taittiriyaka Upanishad, Third Valli, Tenth Anuvaka.

6. Qur'an 4:36–37.

7. Lev. 19:34.

8. Matt. 25:34–36.

9. For my most recent essay on welcoming the stranger in the Christian tradition, see Michael Kinnamon, "Koinonia and Philoxenia: Toward an Expanded Ecumenical Ecclesiology," *Ecumenical Trends* 44, 10 (November 2015): 1–5.

10. "An Open Letter to American Politicians and the American Public," http://www.ciunow.org/wp-content/uploads/2013/08/Three-Religions-Unite-Against-Anti-Muslim-Hate-Rhetoric.pdf.

11. Firmin DeBrabander, *Do Guns Make Us Free?: Democracy and the Armed Society* (New Haven, CT: Yale University Press, 2015), 44.

12. Daniel Bar-Tal, "Why Does Fear Override Hope in Societies Engulfed by Intractable Conflict, as It Does in the Israeli Society?," *Political Psychology* 22, 3 (2001): 601.

13. Gregg Easterbrook, "When Did Optimism Become Uncool?," *New York Times*, May 12, 2016, http://www.nytimes.com/2016/05/15/opinion/sunday/when-did-optimism-become-uncool.html.

14. Zygmunt Bauman, *Liquid Fear* (Cambridge: Polity Press, 2006), 2.

15. Fear has been a building block of totalitarian societies. See Vaclav Havel, *Open Letters: Selected Writings, 1965–1990*, ed. Paul Wilson (New York: Vintage Books, 1992), 52–55. The question is why it is now so prevalent in democratic societies.

16. Bauman, *Liquid Fear*, 129.

17. Ibid. Bauman draws heavily on Robert Castel, *L'insécurité social. Qu'est-ce qu'etre protégé?* (Paris: Sevil, 2003).

18. Peter Stearns, *American Fear: The Causes and Consequences of High Anxiety* (New York and London: Routledge, 2006), 213.

19. Ibid., 214.

20. Ibid., 215.

21. Daniel Gardner, *The Science of Fear* (New York: Plume Book, 2008), 2–3.

22. Stearns, *American Fear*, 216.

23. Langdon Gilkey, "Plurality and Its Theological Implications," in John Hick and Paul F. Knitter, eds., *The Myth of Christian Uniqueness: Toward a Pluralistic Theology of Religions* (Maryknoll, NY: Orbis Books, 1987), 44–45.